H. RICHARD NIEBUHR

Dr. Niebuhr was born in Wright City, Missouri. He is a graduate of Elmhurst College, receiving his B. D. degree at Yale Divinity School and his Ph. D. at Yale University. He was president of Elmhurst College, 1924-1927; professor of the philosophy of religion at Eden Theological Seminary, 1927-1931. He is now professor of Christian Ethics at the Divinity School of Yale University. He is the author of "The Social Sources of Denominationalism," "The Kingdom of God in America," and editor of "The Church Against the World."

THE MEANING OF
REVELATION

THE MACMILLAN COMPANY
NEW YORK · BOSTON · CHICAGO · DALLAS
ATLANTA · SAN FRANCISCO

MACMILLAN AND CO., Limited
LONDON · BOMBAY · CALCUTTA · MADRAS
MELBOURNE

THE MACMILLAN COMPANY
OF CANADA, Limited
TORONTO

THE MEANING
OF REVELATION

by

H. RICHARD NIEBUHR
The Divinity School, Yale University

NEW YORK

THE MACMILLAN COMPANY

1955

Presented to

Douglas Clyde Macintosh

and

Frank Chamberlain Porter

PREFACE

A PREFACE can serve a useful function if it makes the reading of a book easier by directing initial attention to salient problems and ideas and by placing the author and his work in their "existential" setting. The general problem of this essay, indicated by the title, is involved and complex. Among the subsidiary questions which it raises are those about the relations of the relative and the absolute in history, about the connections between "scientific" or objective and religious history, and the perennial problem of natural religion and historical faith. The first of these groups of questions has caused me the greatest concern. We are aware today that all our philosophical ideas, religious dogmas and moral imperatives are historically conditioned and this awareness tempts us to a new agnosticism. I have found myself unable to avoid the acceptance of historical relativism yet I do not believe that the agnostic consequence is necessary. Such relativism calls rather, I believe, for the development of a new type of critical idealism which recognizes the social and historical character of the mind's categories and is "belieffully" realistic, in Professor Tillich's meaning of that phrase. The problem of reconciling a fully independent objective history with a valid religious history has also been approached from a somewhat Kantian point of view by recognizing the difference between pure and practical reason as these deal with history. The problem of natural and revealed religion, finally, has been dealt with as involving neither mutually exclusive principles nor yet distinct stages in a continuous development but rather transformation or conversion, in which the later stage is less the product than the transformer of the previous stage. It may appear then that I have tried to seize both horns of every dilemma with which the problem of Christian faith in history confronted me. But I trust that I have not fallen into paradox.

Among the convictions which in part appear explicitly in this study and in part underlie the argument even where they do not become explicit, three seem to be of fundamental importance, though I may presuppose others of which I am less aware. The first is the conviction that self-defense is the most prevalent source of error in all thinking and perhaps especially in theology and ethics. I cannot hope to have avoided this error in my effort to state Christian ideas in confessional terms only, but I have at least tried to guard against it. The second idea is that the great source of evil in life is the absolutizing of the relative, which in Christianity takes the form of substituting religion, revelation, church or Christian morality for God. The third conviction, which becomes most explicit in the latter part of this essay but underlies the former part, is that Christianity is "permanent revolution" or *metanoia* which does not come to an end in this world, this life, or this time. Positively stated these three convictions are that man is justified by grace, that God is sovereign, and that there is an eternal life.

The book as published contains, with some additions and revisions, the Nathanael W. Taylor Lectures given in the Divinity School of Yale University in April, 1940. Lectures on the same subject, though with somewhat varying content, were given in 1938 and 1939 at Emanuel College in Toronto and at Hebrew Union College in Cincinnati, Ohio. To my colleagues in theology at these institutions, teachers and students alike, particularly to those at Yale, I am deeply indebted for the opportunity and challenge they gave me to develop my thought on the subject of revelation, for the stimulation of theological debate and the encouragement of fellowship in a common quest. The larger debt I owe for whatever ideas in this book may be found to be "for God's greater glory and man's salvation" has been indicated in part in the dedication to two great theologians and teachers. If the relation of my thought to their teaching is not always obvious to the reader, yet my dependence on them and on what I have learned from them is obvious to me. I hope it will be somewhat apparent to them.

Students of theology will recognize that Ernst Troeltsch and Karl Barth have also been my teachers, though only through their writings. These two leaders in twentieth century religious thought are frequently set in diametrical opposition to each other; I have tried to combine their main interests, for it appears to me that the critical thought of the former and the constructive work of the latter belong together. If I have failed the cause does not lie in the impossibility of the task. It is work that needs to be done.

There are, of course, many others—authors, teachers, and colleagues—from whom I have received illumination and guidance; the names of Henri Bergson, A. E. Taylor, Martin Buber, Emil Brunner, Paul Tillich, Robert L. Calhoun, and of my brother Reinhold Niebuhr come immediately to mind; there are many others. With gratitude I record here my obligation to all these and to those non-theological companions who have supported me in my work with other gifts and blessings.

H. RICHARD NIEBUHR

CONTENTS

THE MEANING OF
REVELATION

CHAPTER I

THE POINT OF VIEW

WHAT is the meaning of revelation? The question has been raised many times in the history of the Christian church. But its reappearance in contemporary theological discussion puzzles many men who are accustomed to associate the word revelation with ancient quarrels and their fruitless issue. They remember particularly the turgid debate about miracles, prophecy, revelation and reason in which Deists and Supernaturalists engaged at the beginning of the eighteenth century. The defense of revelation at that time seemed to mean social and intellectual conservatism; what was at stake in the quarrel was the right of the church, clergy, and traditional authority in general to exercise their ancient guardianship over society; the appeal to revelation seemed simply a defensive device. The cause of reason on the other hand was espoused by the rebellious and fresh powers of democratic, mercantile civilization which used it for the attainment of other victories than those of reason. And whatever the fortunes of the contending parties in that conflict were, reason and revelation were sadly damaged. At its close, as at the end of every war, victor and victim were almost indistinguishable. Scepticism, clothed in the episcopal vestments Butler gave it, or in the more worldly armor Hume supplied, was left in possession of the intellectual field.

Yet reason and faith were far from dead; in a little while each recovered some health and in chastened mood turned to its own proper task. With Kant reason acknowledged, as in the sciences it observed, the limits of its rule; within that domain it proceeded to bring order among anarchic ideas, to clear paths through the jungles of superstition and to induce many a plot of nature to yield fruit for human nourishment. If it did not undertake to defend religion neither did it regard the destruction of faith as its mission. On the other hand faith acknowledged that the conflict had been an error, its fears mistaken. One of the leading champions of the cause of revelation, William Law, confessed, "I have been twenty years in the dust of debate, and I have always found that the more books were written in this way of defending the gospel, the more I was furnished with new objections to it." No set of scholastic and logical opinions "were of any significancy towards making the soul of man either an eternal angel of heaven or an eternal devil of hell." With Wesley, Whitefield, Edwards and their associates, Christianity abandoned the defense of revelation as well as the attack on reason; it turned rather to its proper work of preaching the gospel, of exorcising the demons which inhabit human hearts and of guiding souls to fellowship with a holy spirit. Problems of relationship between reason and faith, theology and philosophy, natural and religious experience arose occasionally, of course, but for a while it seemed that a Platonic justice had been established in which each part of the Christian soul and each institution in Christian society minded its own business and made its contribution to the whole without lapsing again into imperialistic adventures. As for "revelation," the word was used sparingly, however much Scriptures and Christian history were employed in the preaching of the gospel.

When we recall that quarrel and its consequences we are tempted to turn away with some distaste from a revival of the revelation idea. Does not the re-establishment of a theology of revelation mean the renewal of a fruitless warfare between faith and reason? Is it not the sign of a retreat to old entrenchments in which only those veterans of a lost cause, the fundamentalists, are interested? To speak of revelation now seems to imply a reversal of the enlightenment in religious thought which began when Schleiermacher asked and answered his rhetorical question to the cultured despisers of faith: "Do you say that you cannot away with miracles, revelation, inspiration? You are right; the time for fairy tales is past." Such a reversal appears to be as impossible as it is undesirable. The work of a hundred and fifty years in theology cannot be ignored; the methods and the fruits of Biblical and historical criticism as well as of natural and social science cannot be so eliminated from men's minds as to allow them to recover the same attitude toward Scriptures which their seventeenth-century forbears had. We may admire the simplicity and directness with which these answered the question about the meaning of revelation by pointing to the Scriptures and may be ready to concede that there was a wisdom in this simplicity which is lacking in our complicated and analytical scholarship. Nevertheless it is evident that we cannot achieve their innocence of vision by wishing for it. When we reflect on these things it appears to us that the revival of revelation theology is not so much reactionary as fanciful. It seems to be part of the general flight of a troubled generation to fairy-tales and to historical romances. As Roman Catholic imagination flees out of the twentieth century into a fabulous thirteenth, so an atavistic Protestantism shuns the ardors of adventure with the social gospel, flees from the problems which historical and psychological criticism have posed for faith and out of dreamy stuff reconstructs a lost Atlantis of early Protestant thought. In any case, whether it be reactionary or fancifully antiquarian, revelation theology seems irrelevant to many modern Christians.

Closer acquaintance, however, with the thought about revelation which is developing in our time does not permit such an interpretation to stand long. If this theology intends reaction it does so in the manner of a revolutionary movement. No great change in political or economic life has ever taken place without a recollection of the past; no new freedom has ever been won without appeal to an old freedom, nor any right established save as an ancient right denied by intervening tyranny. Changes in religious and moral thought also begin with the remembrance of something superficially forgotten, yet real in a transcendent or social mind. In the sense in which a Socrates, calling on Greek youth to remember, or prophets, reminding Israel of a neglected loyalty, or Reformers, returning to the fountains of Christian inspiration, were reactionary—in that sense the new theology of revelation may be reactionary too. But such reaction is the antithesis of a conservatism that seeks to maintain the customs established in a present time. The search in common memory for the great principles which lie back of accustomed ways and of which these are perversions as well as illustrations can be a very radical and pregnant thing.

Something of the same sort appears to be true with respect to the reputed antiquarianism of the theology of revelation. It returns, to be sure, to Paul, Augustine, Luther and Calvin for instruction in Christian faith and there are among its followers unimaginative authoritarians who seem content to repeat the affirmations of these older theologians or to make ancient thought the exclusive object of study. But this does not appear to be the purpose of the leaders of revelation theology. They do not seek so much to understand the great teachers of the past as to understand the reality toward which these directed their attention; the questions which they put to Paul and Calvin are questions which arise out of the experience and the dilemmas of modern Christians, and the answers older theologians give are not uncritically accepted, however great the filial piety of the disciples. The revival of revelation theology is not due to a conscious effort to repristinate ancient ways of thought but to the emergence in our time of a problem similar to that with which the classic theologians dealt.

The problem and the dilemma have been set by historical relativism. What has made the question about revelation a contemporary and pressing question for Christians is the realization that the point of view which a man occupies in regarding religious as well as any other sort of reality is of profound importance. This is doubtless an old conviction but it has been refreshed and given a new relevance by modern experience, especially by historical criticism and the self-criticism of theology.

I. *Historical Relativism and Revelation*

No other influence has affected twentieth century thought more deeply than the discovery of spatial and temporal relativity. The understanding that the spatio-temporal point of view of an observer enters into his knowledge of reality, so that no universal knowledge of things as they are in themselves is possible, so that all knowledge is conditioned by the standpoint of the knower, plays the same rôle in our thinking that the idealistic discoveries of the seventeenth and eighteenth centuries and the evolutionary discovery of the nineteenth played in the thought of earlier generations. That this is true in natural science, particularly in physics, is generally acknowledged; but the physicist's theory of relativity is only one special instance of a far wider and perhaps more important phenomenon, just as Darwin's special theory of biological evolution was an application and development in a restricted sphere of an idea which had an earlier origin and far wider relevance. Theology at all events is concerned with the principle of relativity as this has been demonstrated by history and sociology rather than by physics, and if it is developing into a relativistic theology this is the result not of an effort on its part to keep up with natural science or with the popular linguistic fashions of the day but rather of an attempt to adjust itself to a new self-knowledge.

Earlier idealism, whose critique of religious thought Schleiermacher found himself forced to accept, convinced theology that it could not describe its object directly as though either reason or the Scriptures gave immediate access to divine being; it could only inquire into the reality presented in the complex of psychological experience. Such self-knowledge led theology to adopt the empirical method in its dual form of critical idealism and critical realism. Theology needed to confess its limitations; it could not describe God as he is in himself but only God in human experience; yet it was able to work within those limits with an effectiveness greater if anything than it had possessed before. As a critical theology it could make its careful distinctions between essential and non-essential elements in religious experience, eliminate from consideration all that was purely private and momentary, and furnish to religious life some understanding of itself as well as principles for the guidance of experience and the elimination of error. At the same time it was found that empirical theology left as much room for faith as rationalistic theology—in both its naturalistic and supernatural-istic forms—had done, while the necessity of faith was no less nor greater than before.

The imperative, "Know thyself," is never completely obeyed, but our hesitant compliances do lead to ever new understandings of the limitations as well as of the possibilities of the mind. History and sociology have continued the human self-criticism which psychology began. They have taught us that we are not only beings whose intelligence is conditioned by sensation, interest and feeling and whose limited categories of understanding give limited form and structure to sense-experience, but that we are also beings whose concepts are something less than the categories of a universal reason. Critical idealists and realists knew themselves to be human selves with a specific psychological and logical equipment; their successors know themselves to be social human beings whose reason is not a common reason, alike in all human selves, but one which is qualified by inheritance from a particular society. They know that they are historical selves whose metaphysics, logic, ethics and theology, like their economics, politics and rhetoric are limited, moving and changing in time. This self-knowledge has not come easily to us; we have resisted it and continue to avoid it when we can, but the cumulative evidence of history and sociology continue to impress upon us, against our desire, the conviction that our reason is not only in space-time but that time-space is in our reason. The patterns and models we employ to understand the historical world may have had a heavenly origin, but as we know and use them they are, like ourselves, creatures of history and time; though we direct our thought to eternal and transcendent beings, it is not eternal and transcendent; though we regard the universal, the image of the universal in our mind is not a universal image.

How true this is, in such areas of inquiry as economics and politics, historical criticism has taught all but the most dogmatic devotees of doctrine to recognize. Great phrases such as "the natural rights of men," "the natural order," "the system of natural liberty," "the divine right of kings," "the law of supply and demand," and "the iron law of wages," with which rationalism in politics and economics operated, now appear to us to be neither intuitions of a pure reason, nor deductions from absolute premises, nor inductions from universal experience, but rather intuitions of historically conditioned and temporal reasons, or deductions from relative premises, or inductions from limited historical and social experience. Doubtless they refer to objective relations; doubtless too they were and largely remain useful instruments for the analysis of actual relations between men; but we discern in all such formulations elements which are thoroughly relative to historical background, to a will to believe, and to the specific interests of certain social groups.

What is true of the much abused sciences of economic and political life is no less true of those types of thought which have acquired a certain specious sanctity from their association with the temples in which men worship and with the separated, philosophic life. We note that relativism appears in ethics as it does in politics—not only the psychological relativism with which the great schools of rational morality have always tried to come to grips but the historical relativism to which these schools are themselves subject. The great conception of duty which Kant discovered as the rational essence of universal moral experience appears to the historical view to be essence only of any practical reason which has been educated, as Kant's had been, in a society in which the Judaic-Christian tradition is predominant. We need not doubt that the categorical imperative contains a universal meaning but Kant's formulations of it are historically relative and when we, in our later historical period, attempt to reformulate the Kantian thought we also do so as historically conditioned thinkers who cannot describe the universal save from a relative point of view. If Kant's ethics must be historically understood, no less must the Utilitarianism of Bentham and John Stuart Mill be interpreted against the background of English social history. Though Bentham begins with an experience so universally human as pleasure, the place he assigns to this good, the way in which he develops his hedonic calculus, the manner in which he makes this ethics a basis for law-making, are all evidently dependent on the relative situation of an eighteenth century British reason. In like manner Epicurean hedonism is Hellenistic, being in many ways more akin to its Stoic opponent in history than to its Utilitarian successor, as the latter is more closely related to the idealism of its day than to the hedonisms of other times. So also the social and historical sources of Plato's, Aristotle's and Spinoza's ethics are not less important than those of the customary moralities of non-literary peoples. Many philosophers still seek to avoid such knowledge of themselves and their enterprise; they may employ the historical or the psychological method when they criticize opposing systems of thought but wish to except their own ideas from the rule of historical relativity. To the rest of us, however, their abstractions are unintelligible save as we consciously or unconsciously share their historical and social point of view.

Metaphysics, and doubtless logic and epistemology, are as historical as ethics. In every field of philosophical enquiry the historical approach has established itself. Its employment means that men realize that they cannot understand what others are trying to communicate by words and signs unless they try first of all to occupy the same standpoint, to look in the same direction and to use the same instruments of measurement and analysis, subject to the same conditions, as those which the original observer occupies, regards and uses. Locke and the empiricists in general understood that experience provided the limits within which reason must work, but we are required in our time to recognize the further fact that the reason which operates in this restricted field is itself limited by its historical and social character.

It is not enough to say that men live in time and must conceive all things as temporal and historical. Doubtless it is true that all reality has become temporal for us. But our historical relativism affirms the historicity of the subject even more than that of the object; man, it points out, is not only in time but time is in man. Moreover and more significantly, the time that is in man is not abstract but particular and concrete; it is not a general category of time but rather the time of a definite society with distinct language, economic and political relations, religious faith and social organization. How such particular historical time works in man has been indicated more precisely in connection with economic history than with any other. The hypothesis of Marx and Engels in its extremer form is overstated but its critical application by careful scholars to social history has yielded results which no one who takes human self-knowledge seriously can easily discount. The point of such Marxian analysis is that men are deeply influenced in all their thinking and acting, not simply by the fact that they are economic men with the common human desire for temporal goods, but rather men living amid certain, definite economic relations, who think as pastoral, agricultural, industrial, or bourgeois men. In similar fashion the philosophy and sociology of language indicate how time is in man. They are beginning to make clear what has been known in part since the ways of right thought were called logical—that word and idea are inseparable, that language conditions thought. But language is always particular and historical, never general and static. Without a universal language there can be no universal thought, though every particular language expresses ideas about universals.

Theologians have probably been reminded even more frequently and effectively than economists, political scientists and philosophers, of the relativity of their point of view. If they were Biblical theologians, who made the Bible not only the object of their inquiry but also sought to take the Biblical standpoint, they discovered that the latter was historically and socially conditioned. They found that an interpretation of the words of Jesus made from the historical standpoint of nineteenth century liberal thought could not be fair to the content of his message; but to take their standpoint in the first century and to think with Jesus was to think also as historically conditioned beings with Rabbinic, prophetic and apocalyptic ideas in mind. If the theologian was a rationalist, relying on the dogmas of common sense, he learned that the latter is exactly what the phrase indicates—the sense of a community—and that every community is a particular thing, the product of its own past and the possessor of a limited culture. Just as the great truths of political and economic rationalism are now recognized to be infected with historicity and relativity so the great innate ideas of religious rationalism are known to be innate in men of a certain historical culture rather than in men in general. It was said of a German philosopher of religion that he regarded as innate truths of reason all the ideas he had learned before he was five years old; the statement is more or less applicable to all men. Rationalism always works with ideas that it takes for granted, but what is granted to it comes through an historical medium. If the theologian was an empiricist who used a particular scheme of categories or a particular value-scale for the analysis of religious experience, as a scientist uses mathematics, he was reminded that categorical schemes and value-scales have a history, as mathematical systems have, or that they are dependent on intuitions which are those of historical, temporal men. Whether they are also the schemes and scales of a universal reason cannot be determined by reference to their apparent innateness, clarity or inescapability, since the ideas commonly accepted in a society always appear to its members to be self-evident and inevitable. Finally, the creedal theologians, who began with the dogmas of the church, found themselves in like condemnation with their fellows, since the historical origin of the creeds and the historical background of the creeds' interpreters could not be ignored. There does not seem then to be any apparent possibility of escape from the dilemma of historical relativism for any type of theology. The historical point of view of the observer must be taken into consideration in every case since no observer can get out of history into a realm beyond time-space; if reason is to operate at all it must be content to work as an historical reason.

In this situation many old and new temptations arise. As reason confined to experience seemed to lose all confidence in itself with Hume, so a sceptical historical relativism today proclaims the unreliability of all thought conditioned by historical and social background. On the other hand, as subjective idealism sought to overcome the limitations which empiricism had brought to light by exalting the subjective as alone real, so national, racial and ecclesiastical relativism proclaims that only the thought and experience of a particular historical group is true and dependable. Our social solipsism —expressed in practice even more than in theory— is the modern counterpart of individualistic subjectivism. With these dangers confronting thought, it is not strange that men today seek to avoid the problem by damning historical relativism itself as an aberration. In the earlier period, however, despite the flamboyancy of sceptical despair and the imperial exuberance of subjectivism, the work of reason was carried on by those refused to retreat to pre-empirical positions while yielding neither to the temptation of rational suicide in scepticism or of egoistic totalitarianism. Critical philosophy and critical theology accepted the limitations imposed on the rational subject by a new self-knowledge and undertook the apparently humble task of criticizing, interpreting and guiding experience with the aid of limited principles. So in our time the recognition of reason's historical limitations can be for theology in particular, as for the social sciences in general, the prelude to faithful critical work in history and in historically apprehended experience.

A critical historical theology cannot, to be sure, prescribe what form religious life must take in all places and all times beyond the limits of its own historical system. But it can seek within the history of which it is a part for an intelligible pattern; it can undertake to analyze the reason which is in that history and to assist those who participate in this historical life to disregard in their thinking and practice all that is secondary and not in conformity with the central ideas and patterns of the historical movement. Such theology can attempt to state the grammar, not of a universal religious language, but of a particular language, in order that those who use it may be kept in true communication with each other and with the realities to which the language refers. It may try to develop a method applicable not to all religions but to the particular faith to which its historical point of view is relevant. Such theology in the Christian church cannot, it is evident, be an offensive or defensive enterprise which undertakes to prove the superiority of Christian faith to all other faiths; but it can be a confessional theology which carries on the work of self-criticism and self-knowledge in the church.

More than this is required of and possible to a theology of historical relativism. Relativism does not imply subjectivism and scepticism. It is not evident that the man who is forced to confess that his view of things is conditioned by the standpoint he occupies must doubt the reality of what he sees. It is not apparent that one who knows that his concepts are not universal must also doubt that they are concepts of the universal, or that one who understands how all his experience is historically mediated must believe that nothing is mediated through history. The recognition of man's natural equality in the eighteenth century was not the recognition of an untruth because the way in which relations between men were apprehended and expressed was relative to the historical standpoint of the time. So long as we occupy the same general standpoint, that is so long as we participate in the same historical process in which the early democrats participated, we shall be able to look at the same aspect of the universal which they saw and to conceive and express what we see in terms something like their own. It is not filial piety which convinces us of the truth of their statement and it is not superior intelligence which convinces racialists of our time that natural equality is a myth. Conviction of the truth in the idea of human equality grows out of a communication with reality as it is visible from the point of view of our common social history. It is true that we cannot see this relation between men if we take the standpoint of ancient Greek civilization or that of modern racialism; from such points of view we shall see only differences and inequalities; but what we see from the democratic point of view is really there, even though all men do not see it and even though our way of expressing it is not a universal way.

The acceptance of the reality of what we see in psychological and historically conditioned experi-

ence is always something of an act of faith; but such
faith is inevitable and justifies itself or is justified
by its fruits. A critical idealism is always accompanied, openly or disguisedly, by a critical realism
which accepts on faith the independent reality of
what is mediated through sense, though it discrim-
inates between uninterpreted and unintelligible
impressions and verifiable, constant, intelligible
content. As an empirical science operates with
animal faith in the reality of the objects which it
searches out and mates its doubts of impressionistic
experience with confidence in the objectivity of
experience's core, so an historical relativism can and
must proceed with faith in the midst of all its criticism of historical subjects and objects mediated
through history. If we are confined by our situation to the knowledge of God which is possible to
those who live in Christian history we are not
thereby confined to a knowledge of Christian history but in faith can think with Christianity about
God, and in Christianity have experience of the
being who is the beginning and the end of this
historic faith.

Furthermore historic faith, directed toward a
reality which appears in our history and which is
apprehended by historic beings, is not private and
subjective, without possibility of verification. To
be in history is to be in society, though in a particular society. Every view of the universal from the

finite standpoint of the individual in such a society is subject to the test of experience on the part of companions who look from the same standpoint in the same direction as well as to the test of consistency with the principles and concepts that have grown out of past experience in the same community. A theology which undertakes the limited work of understanding and criticizing within Christian history the thought and action of the church is also a theology which is dependent on the church for the constant test of its critical work. Being in social history it cannot be a personal and private theology nor can it live in some non-churchly sphere of political or cultural history; its home is the church; its language is the language of the church; and with the church it is directed toward the universal from which the church knows itself to derive its being and to which it points in all its faith and works.

Finally, historical relativism also means relevance to history. Empiricism limited reason to experience but it also showed the relevance of reason to experience and led to the rationalization of experience. So historical relativism, acknowledging the limitation of religious reason to history, can cherish the hope that work in the limited sphere may issue in better intellectual and practical organization of the historical, social life of Christianity.

Theology, then, must begin in Christian history

and with Christian history because it has no other choice; in this sense it is forced to begin with revelation, meaning by that word simply historic faith. But such a limited beginning is a true beginning and not the end of inquiry; it is a point of view and not the eclipse of a once illuminated scene. When a theology that has been convinced of its historical relativism speaks of revelation it means not only that in religion, as in other affairs, men are historically conditioned but also that to the limited point of view of historic Christian faith a reality discloses itself which invites all the trust and devotion of finite, temporal men. Such a theology of revelation is objectively relativistic, proceeding with confidence in the independent reality of what is seen, though recognizing that its assertions about that reality are meaningful only to those who look upon it from the same standpoint.

This is the first reason why the question about the meaning of revelation has become important in our time. To speak of revelation now is not to retreat to modes of thought established in earlier generations but to endeavor to deal faithfully with the problem set for Christians in our time by the knowledge of our historical relativity.

II. *Religious Relativism and Revelation*

Another and more ancient dilemma forces modern theology to begin with revelation. Briefly stated it is this, that one can speak and think significantly about God only from the point of view of faith in him. Knowledge of this second limitation of theological reason doubtless goes very far back into Christian and Jewish history, but we need remind ourselves only of the more recent recognitions of its actuality and of the way in which theological self-criticism has enforced the conviction in modern times.

At the beginning of the modern era Luther vigorously and repeatedly affirmed that God and faith belonged together so that all statements about God which are made from some other point of view than that of faith in him are not really statements about him at all. "What does it mean to have a god," he asked, "or what is God?" And the answer was that "trust and faith of the heart alone make both God and idol. . . . For the two, faith and God, hold close together. Whatever then thy heart clings to . . . and relies upon, that is properly thy god." The great empirical theology of the nineteenth century was at least partly based on the renewal of this understanding. Both Schleiermacher and Ritschl owed no small part of their success to their observance of the limitation of theology to the point of view of faith in the God of Jesus Christ. The former saw that the God whom theology could describe in its very inadequate fashion was a being who was the counterpart of that subjective trust

which he defined as the feeling of absolute dependence and never a being who could be mated
with feelings of relative dependence and relative
freedom. It was Schleiermacher's knowledge of
the inseparability of God and faith quite as much
as his idealism which led him to reject the speculative method in theology and to approach his subject through the pious feelings of the religious man.
It is necessary, he contended, to keep the feeling
of absolute dependence and God together because
otherwise one will speak about the world instead
of about God. We may paraphrase him in this
fashion: the being we talk about in Christianity is,
whatever else he is, a value and absolute value, that
is a being on whom the self feels wholly dependent
for any worth as well as any existence it possesses.
Now we cannot begin to speak about a being who
is absolute value by talking first of all about some
being which has no value or which is dependent
on us for its value. Schleiermacher refrained from
making the apologetic statement that we are never
bare of some sense of personal value-relation so
that when we speak about something on which we
are not absolutely dependent we necessarily speak
of something that is partly dependent on us. He
recognized the fact but confined himself to faith;
it was not the business of theology to transcend its
limits as a theology of faith. It had enough to do
in this area; God and faith belong together. "There

are many," wrote he, "who, confident of the fact that they possess an original idea of God, wholly independent of all feeling, reject the feeling of absolute dependence as something almost sub-human. Our statement does not wish to challenge such an original knowledge of God but only set it aside as something with which we can have nothing to do in Christian theology since evidently it has no immediate connection with piety."

Ritschl carried on this relational value-theology in a form which has become very familiar. His treatment was based on the recognition that Christian affirmations about God, sin, Christ, salvation, etc., are meaningful only in a Christian context, or—to state the idea in the broader way in which he put it—religious judgments are value-judgments which report not simply experience but value-experience in which there has been a response of the whole feeling, willing, desiring person. When a Christian says "God" he does not mean that a being exists who is the beginning of the solar system or of the cosmos, or the great mathematician who figured out a world in which mathematicians can take delight. What he means, what he points to with the word "God," is a being infinitely attractive, which by its very nature calls forth devotion, joy and trust. This God is always "my God," "our Good," "our beginning" and "our end." To speak about God otherwise, in the first place at least,

would be like speaking about beauty in a picture
to which one did not respond with delight, as
though color and texture and balance, just as they
are in themselves or impersonally considered, were
beauty. Ritschl's insistence on the valuational character of Christian concepts and judgments helped
to clear up many confused and confusing points in
Christian thought. It indicated why the intellect-
ualistic approach in theology always remained re-
ligiously unsatisfactory, why it led away from the
religious community, why it tended to bring forth
neither prayer nor repentance, neither adoration
nor reformation. He helped also by means of this
approach, as Schleiermacher had done before him,
to clear up the discrepancies between religious and
non-religious views of the same event. As Schleiermacher had pointed out, "the strange question
whether the same statement can be true in philosophy and untrue in theology, or vice versa, can
no longer arise for the reason that the statement
as it occurs in the one can find no place in the
other and, alike as they may sound, their difference must always be presupposed." The renewal
of the faith method in theology had other important consequences: it gave impetus to the historical examination of Christian faith, since scholarship was encouraged to seek the bases of that faith
in Christian life itself rather than in idealistic or
other philosophic dogma; it re-enforced the inter-

est of Christians in the historic Jesus and in his religious faith; it provided strength for the growing social gospel and invigorated the moral life of the church. The fruits which this faith-theology produced gave some evidence of the correctness of its method.

But if the test of a method is to be found in its results then the empirical faith-theology of Schleiermacher and Ritschl must not only be praised for its good consequences but blamed for the misconceptions to which it gave rise and which revealed their fallaciousness in the experience of the church. Today an ungrateful generation of theologians, owing far more to its predecessors than it acknowledges, delights in pointing out the evil which lives after Schleiermacher while it inters his good with his bones. Yet there is justice in its criticism, however unjust its pride, for Schleiermacher apparently was betrayed into an inconsistency in his method which brought fateful consequences with it. Though he acknowledged the togetherness of God and the feeling of absolute dependence so that one could not speak of the former save from the point of view of the latter yet he did not really take this standpoint in his theology but made the feeling of absolute dependence his object, so directing the attention of faith toward itself rather than toward God. Schleiermacher, indeed, was far less subjectivistic than many of his followers who used the sin of the father as an occasion for committing sins of their own. Nevertheless his faith-theology became a "faithology" or a "religionology" which turned attention away from God to religious feelings and tended to make the religious consciousness the object of confidence. The temptation is one to which all Protestant theology since the time of Luther has been subject. In Lutheranism the subjectivistic inversion manifested itself in the tendency to ascribe saving power to faith itself rather than to the God of faith and in Schleiermacher's successors it appeared in the ascription to religion of all the attributes which religion itself would ascribe to God. Religion became for them the enhancer of life, the creator of spiritual and social energy, the redeemer of man from evil, the builder of the beloved community, the integrator of the great spiritual values; the God of religion, however, came to be a necessary auxiliary, though it could be questioned whether a real God was necessary to religion or only a vivid idea of God. The term "religionist" which has been invented in modern times applies aptly to those who follow the tendency inaugurated in part by Schleiermacher, for religion is the object of concern and the source of strength for them rather than the God whom an active faith regards as alone worthy of supreme devotion. This tendency in religion is the counterpart of the inversions which take place in other areas in which

value-relations are made ultimate values; so aesthet-
icism values aesthetic feelings rather than beau-
tiful objects and moralism makes virtue in the self
rather than the good toward which a virtuous life
is directed the object of its concern.

Ritschl's theology of faith went astray at a
slightly different point than Schleiermacher's and
became inconsistent in more explicit fashion. After
all his insistence that "one can recognize and understand God, sin, conversion, eternal life in a Christian sense only insofar as one consciously and
purposefully counts oneself a member of the community which Christ founded," and in spite of his
criticism of traditional theological method as inconsistent because it jumped from a standpoint outside of Christianity to a standpoint in Christianity,
from natural theology to revelation, without
awareness of the leap, Ritschl also began to analyze
God's nature simply from the point of view of a
member of the human community confronting
nature. Having said that Christian judgments are
value-judgments he proceeded to set forth a value-
scale which was not that of Christian faith, for
which God is the highest value and could not be
God were he not absolute in worth, but was rather
the value-scale of civilized man. His value-standard
is well known: "The religious view of things rests
on the fact that man distinguishes himself in worth
from the phenomena around him"; "in every re-

ligion what is sought with the help of superhuman, spiritual power, reverenced by man, is a solution of the contradiction in which man finds himself as both a part of nature and a spiritual personality claiming to dominate nature." Having said originally that God, as known in Christianity, can only be spoken of as he appears to one who responds to him with feeling and will, he now posits a human will and desire directed not toward God but toward the maintenance of man's superiority over nature; so he interprets the value of God to man through man's evaluation of himself as this appears in his self-comparison not with God but with nature. Ritschl did not do what many value-theorists do—abstract the concept of value from the relation of man to other persons or things in which desiring man finds value or disvalue. But having said that the relation of man to God is a value-relation he posited a prior value-relation—man in opposition to nature. In relation to nature man values himself; he can without too much difficulty regard himself as the crown of natural development; he values nature as that which serves his own worth; it is instrumental to him; it is something he dominates. So Ritschl approached God not from the point of view of Christian faith which values God as infinitely superior to man and the source of whatever real value man himself has, but rather from the standpoint of man's confidence in his own worth as superior to nature. Hence the deity Ritschl began to speak of was again not the God of Christian faith but the being or beings which support man's confidence in himself as a supernatural being. This deity was an instrument, not an end; it was the counterpart of man's sense of freedom not of his sense of absolute dependence; it was the reality—whatever it might be—which supported man's sense of his own intrinsic value. Such faith was directed not toward the God of Christianity but "toward the supernatural independence of the spirit in all its relations to the world of nature and to society."

The sources of Ritschl's value-scale can be traced back infinitely far into history. Greeks, in their classic no less than in their Sophistic thought, made man the measure of all things and always used the value-scale derived from a comparison of man with so-called lower animals for the measurement of all other relations. In Ritschl's case the immediate historical source was evidently Kantian philosophy. But it is unnecessary as well as unavailing for theology to make Greek thought or philosophy its constant scapegoat. The inversion of faith whereby man puts himself into the center, constructs an anthropocentric universe and makes confidence in his own value rather than faith in God his beginning has occurred over and over again in the past and will doubtless occur many times in the future. It is often accomplished with the aid of philosophy but it can be accomplished with the help of Scriptures, as when in interpreting the account of creation in Genesis man's dominion over nature is put prior to his dependence on the Creator. It can be accomplished with the aid of some revealed law or gospel; occasions differ but the tendency is universal. What led Ritschl to his departure from his professed standpoint of Christian faith in God and so to inconsistency in his theology and the misdirection of Christian life was, as the context of his argument indicates, a desire to justify Christianity as the best religion. Schleiermacher's inversion also seems to have been largely due to his desire to defend religion as an important element in human spiritual life. Ritschl, at all events, though he began with the endeavor to help Christians become good Christians and the church a good church allowed himself to be diverted toward the wholly different effort to prove that Christians, as Christians, were somehow better than other men and that Christianity was the best religion. This he could not do save by reference to some element which Christianity seemed to have in common with other faiths and in which it excelled; so he dropped the standpoint of Christian faith which makes the God of Jesus Christ the measure of all things and took up the standpoint of faith in man as a being superior to nature; in this faith man is the measure of all things. It was defensiveness and the desire to prove the worth of Christianity otherwise than this might be proved or disproved by the fruits of Christian faith that tempted Ritschl to relinquish the standpoint of faith in God and to accept the point of view of pagan confidence in man.

The consequences of the Ritschlian aberration are well known, though again it is with doubtful right that theological children blame their fathers for having eaten sour grapes. Ritschl with his double point of view saw double. Christianity was for him not a circle centering in God but an ellipse with two foci—God before whom man is a forgiven sinner, who is for man the beginning of all things, and man who, confronting nature, regards himself as beginning and end in a kingdom of ends. For Ritschl's successors Christianity often became an affair of two exclusive circles, one of religion so-called and one of so-called ethics; and sometimes it became a single circle centering in man's spiritual personality, God or an idea of God being somewhere at the circumference. What was worse than the confusion this brought to theology was the uncertainty it imported into the church which was placed in the strange dilemma of becoming either a kind of special institution for the cultivation of religious sensibilities or an ethical culture society for the promotion of man's dominion over nature, human and otherwise.

Schleiermacher and Ritschl cannot be blamed, of course, for all the consequences which have followed from the inconsistencies of their faith-theologies. In part they were but representative men who illustrated in their theories tendencies which were more pronounced in the actual life of the church than in the theories. Moreover Christianity seized on the opportunities offered by the leaders of thought to abandon the standpoint of Christian faith and to take up another point of view. Christians were tempted in the nineteenth and twentieth centuries, perhaps more than in most previous times, to consider themselves first of all as members of national and cultural societies rather than of the church and to turn Christian faith into an auxiliary of civilization. But the temptation and the tendency to anthropocentrism are universal and one may be very sure that any new theology—the theology of revelation for instance—will be subject to the same perversion and will not fail to offer opportunities for it. For faith in the God of Jesus Christ is a rare thing and faith in idols tends forever to disguise itself as Christian trust.

Our present concern, however, is not with the religious and moral consequences but with the theological aspects of this situation. Consistency in theology is certainly an ideal to be espoused, whatever difficulties may stand in the way of its realization, and consistency here as in every rational inquiry means adherence to a single point of view. Furthermore, theology has been taught by many sad experiences that the only point of view from which the God of Christian faith may be understood is that of Christian faith itself. The situation is not a strange one in human knowledge. The sciences of nature have learned that if they are to proceed with their proper work it is necessary for them to be single-minded, directing their attention to their objects, developing methods corresponding to those objects, and not diverting attention from nature to super-nature or changing their standpoint from single-minded observation to the interestedness of men concerned about the value of science itself or ·about the victory of some proletarian, democratic or religious cause. A theology which abandons the point of view of faith in God does not do so, as the examples of Schleiermacher and Ritschl indicate, because that point of view is too interested but because it does not permit theology to follow another interest—the defense of the value of Christianity itself or of religion or of civilization or of man. Whatever be the case in other human inquiries there is no such thing as disinterestedness in theology, since one cannot speak of God and gods at all save as valued beings or as values which cannot be apprehended save by a willing, feeling, responding self. Theology may try to maintain the standpoint of Christian faith, that is of an interest directed as exclusively as possible to the God of Christian faith; or it may take the position of faith in some other being, that is of an interest directed more or less exclusively toward religion, or toward the moral consciousness, or toward man's own worth, or toward civilization. When it follows one of these latter interests it does not become more disinterested and objective than when it takes the point of view of Christian faith; it simply becomes primarily interested in something that faith in God must regard as too narrow and finite to be a substitute for the Father of Jesus Christ. And when such theology turns to the latter being from the point of view of its dominant faith in another valued entity it does not really turn to the Christian God at all as Christian faith knows him, but rather to some instrumental value which serves its major interest. The god who is primarily a helper toward the attainment of human wishes is not the being to whom Christ said, "Thy will, not mine, be done."

The recognition of this situation, as it has developed out of theological self-criticism to a large part, requires modern Christian theology to begin again with the faith of the Christian community and so with revelation. It is necessary to begin where Schleiermacher and Ritschl began for the same reasons that prompted them and not to begin where they left off with the acceptance of all their inconsistencies. To be sure, no modern theologian needs to deceive himself about his ability to evade that rule of original sin, the tendency toward idolatry, which has manifested itself in all the theology of the past; but if he begins with the particular sins of the past and does not make the resolute attempt to start in and with faith in God there is no hope for him and his endeavor.

The theology of revelation as it is developing in our time is the consequence of this understanding of theology's religious relativity as well as of its understanding of historical relativity. If the historical limitations of all thought about God demand that theology begin consciously with and in an historical community, its limitations as an inquiry into the nature of the object of faith require it to begin in faith and therefore in a particular faith, since there is no other kind. Because God and faith belong together the standpoint of the Christian theologian must be in the faith of the Christian community, directed toward the God of Jesus Christ. Otherwise his standpoint will be that of some other community with another faith and another god. There is no neutral standpoint and no faithless situation from which approach can be made to that which is inseparable from faith. Whatever freedom the Christian and the theologian may have, there is no absolute freedom for them in the sense of complete uncommittedness to any supreme value. Neutrality and uncommittedness are great delusions where God and the gods of men are concerned. Men must raise the question about revelation today because the religious as well as the historical bondage of theological reason has become evident again, but also because the freedom of inquiry that is present in this bondage is very real.

III. *Revelation and Confessional Theology*

Beginnings are important but the way pursued is no less important. Theology finds itself forced to begin in historic faith because there is no other starting point for its endeavor. Yet deflections from the straight line that leads from the point of view of a common faith to the object of that faith are as common in theologies of revelation as in any other types of religious thought. The major cause of such aberrations is doubtless the same one which was responsible for the departure from the straight line that occurred in Schleiermacher's and Ritschl's thought—it is the tendency to self-defense and self-justification, the turning away from the object of faith to the subject.

The justification of the Christian, or of the church, or of religion, or of the gospel, or of revelation seems forever necessary in the face of the attacks which are made upon these from the outside and in view of the doubts that arise within. Fear of defeat and loss turn men away from single-minded devotion to their ends in order that they may defend themselves and their means of attaining their ends. We not only employ methods for the discovery of truths but somehow feel it necessary to show, otherwise than by the fruits of our work, that these methods are the best. We not only desire to live in Christian faith but we endeavor to recommend ourselves by means of it and to justify it as superior to all other faiths. Such defense may be innocuous when it is strictly subordinated to the main task of living toward our ends, but put into the first place it becomes more destructive of religion, Christianity and the soul than any foe's attack can possibly be.

A theology of revelation which begins with the historic faith of the Christian community is no less tempted to self-justification and so to abandonment of its starting point than any other theology. It may seek to make a virtue out of its necessity and to recommend itself as not only inescapable but as superior in results to all other methods. It may direct attention away from the God visible to the community of faith and seek to defend that community, its faith and its theology. The idea of revelation itself may be employed, not for the greater glory of God, but as a weapon for the defense and aggrandizement of the church or even of the individual theologian. A recent book on the subject of revelation states that "the question of revelation is at the very root of the claim of the Christian religion to universal empire over the souls of men." Such an apologetic statement contains an evident inherent self-contradiction; for revelation and the "claim of the Christian religion to universal empire over the souls of men" are absolute incompatibles. The faith of Christian revelation is directed toward a God who reveals himself as the only universal sovereign and as the one who judges all men—but particularly those directed to him in faith—to be sinners wholly unworthy of sovereignty. To substitute the sovereignty of Christian religion for the sovereignty of the God of Christian faith, though it be done by means of the revelation idea, is to fall into a new type of idolatry, to abandon the standpoint of Christian faith and revelation which are directed toward the God of Jesus Christ and to take the standpoint of a faith directed toward religion or revelation. A revelation that can be used to undergird the claim of Christian faith to universal empire over the souls of men must be something else than the revelation of the God of that Jesus Christ who in faith emptied himself, made himself of no reputation and refused to claim the kingly crown.

The inherent self-contradiction in all such self-defensive uses of the revelation idea indicates that every effort to deal with the subject must be resolutely confessional. As we begin with revelation only because we are forced to do so by our limited standpoint in history and faith so we can proceed only by stating in simple, confessional form what has happened to us in our community, how we came to believe, how we reason about things and what we see from our point of view.

Other considerations also warn against the apologetic use of revelation and make necessary the adoption of a confessional method. Whenever the revelation idea is used to justify the church's claims to superior knowledge or some other excellence, revelation is necessarily identified with something that the church can possess. Such possessed revelation must be a static thing and under the human control of the Christian community—a book, a creed, or a set of doctrines. It cannot be revelation in act whereby the church itself is convicted of its poverty, its sin and misery before God. Furthermore, it cannot be the revelation of a living God; for the God of a revelation that can be possessed must be a God of the past, a God of the dead who communicated his truths to men in another time but who to all effects and purposes has now retired from the world, leaving the administration of his interests to some custodian of revelation—a church, a priesthood, or a school of theology. Revelation as a contemporary event is then solely a function of this teaching group. There seems to be no way of avoiding such static and deistic interpretations of the revelation idea—interpretations which contradict what is said to be affirmed in revelation, that God is a living God and reveals himself—save by the acceptance of the confessional form of theology. Finally, the confessional form is made necessary by a revelation which exposes human sin no less than divine goodness. A revelation which leaves man without defense before God cannot be dealt with except in confessor's terms. Religious response to revelation is made quite as much in a confession of sin as in a confession of faith and a theology which recognizes that it cannot speak about the content of revelation without accepting the standpoint of faith must also understand that it cannot deal with its object save as sinners' rather than saints' theology. As it is then with the starting point in revelation so it is with the confessional form of theology; necessity, not free choice, determines the acceptance of the way.

This is the sum of the matter: Christian theology must begin today with revelation because it knows that men cannot think about God save as historic, communal beings and save as believers. It must ask what revelation means for Christians rather than what it ought to mean for all men, everywhere and at all times. And it can pursue its inquiry only by recalling the story of Christian life and by analyzing what Christians see from their limited point of view in history and faith.

CHAPTER II

THE STORY OF OUR LIFE

I. *The Historical Method of Christian Faith*

OUR self-consciously historical time accepts the limitations of the historical point of view with a sense of constraint and an air of resignation. In this situation, however, we do well to remind ourselves that the Christian community has usually—and particularly in times of its greatest vigor—used an historical method. Apparently it felt that to speak in confessional terms about the events that had happened to it in its history was not a burdensome necessity but rather an advantage and that the acceptance of an historical point of view was not confining but liberating. The preaching of the early Christian church was not an argument for the existence of God nor an admonition to follow the dictates of some common human conscience, unhistorical and super-social in character. It was primarily a simple recital of the great events connected with the historical appearance of Jesus Christ and a confession of what had happened to the community of disciples. Whatever it was that the church meant to say, whatever was revealed or manifested to it could be indicated only in connection with an historical person and events in the life of his community. The confession referred to history and was consciously made in history.

It is true that when Paul succumbed to his unconquerable tendency to commend himself, he spoke of revelation in private visions; when he attempted to defend himself against the assumption of superiority by Corinthian spiritualists he referred to mysteries and hidden wisdom. But when he went about his proper work of demonstrating to his hearers and readers what he really meant he did so in the following fashion:

I declare unto you the gospel which I preached unto you, which also ye have received and wherein ye stand; by which also ye are saved, if ye keep in memory what I preached unto you, unless ye have believed in vain. For I delivered unto you first of all that which I also received, how that Christ died for our sins according to the scriptures; and that he was buried, and that he rose again the third day according to the scriptures; and that he was seen of Cephas and then of the twelve: after that he was seen of above five hundred brethren at once; of whom the greater part remain unto this present, but some are fallen asleep. After that he was seen of James; then of all the apostles. And last of all he was seen of me also, as of one born out of due time.

The great anonymous theologian of the second century spoke in parables of Hellenic wisdom about the gospel of divine grace; but he could indicate what he meant by the Logos, the Light, and the Life only by telling again in his own way the story of Jesus Christ. The sermons of Peter and Stephen as reported or reconstructed in the book of Acts were recitals of the great events in Christian and Israelite history. Christian evangelism in general, as indicated by the preservation of its material in the Synoptic gospels, began directly with Jesus and told in more or less narrative fashion about those things "which are most surely believed among us" "of all that Jesus began both to do and to teach." We may remind ourselves also of the fact that despite many efforts to set forth Christian faith in metaphysical and ethical terms of great generality the only creed which has been able to maintain itself in the church with any approach to universality consists for the most part of statements about events.

We can imagine that early preachers were often asked to explain what they meant with their talk about God, salvation and revelation, and when they were hard pressed, when all their parables or references to the unknown God and to the Logos, had succeeded only in confusing their hearers they turned at last to the story of their life, saying, "What we mean is this event which happened among us and to us." They followed in this respect the prophets who had spoken of God before them and the Jewish community which had also talked of revelation. These, too, always spoke of history, of what had happened to Abraham, Isaac and Jacob, of a deliverance from Egypt, of the covenant of Sinai, of mighty acts of God. Even their private visions were dated, as "in the year that King Uzziah died," even the moral law was anchored to an historical event, and even God was defined less by his metaphysical and moral character than by his historical relations, as the God of Abraham, Isaac and Jacob.

Interpretation of our meaning with the aid of a story is a well-known pedagogical device. So Lincoln told his homely tales and conveyed to others in trenchant fashion the ideas in his mind; so Plato employed myths to illustrate philosophy and to communicate visions of truth that ordinary language could not describe; so Jesus himself through parables tried to indicate what he meant by the phrase "kingdom of God." Yet what prompted Christians in the past to confess their faith by telling the story of their life was more than a need for vivid illustration or for analogical reasoning. Their story was not a parable which could be replaced by another; it was irreplaceable and untranslatable. An internal compulsion rather than free choice led them to speak of what they knew by telling about Jesus Christ and their relation to God through him.

Today we think and speak under the same compulsion. We find that we must travel the road

which has been taken by our predecessors in the
Christian community, though our recognition of
the fact is first of all only a consequence of the
obstruction of all other ways. We must do what
has been done because we have discovered with
Professor Whitehead that "religions commit suicide when they find their inspiration in their
dogmas. The inspiration of religion lies in the history of religion." Whether this be true of other
faiths than Christianity we may not be sure, but it
seems very true of our faith. Metaphysical systems
have not been able to maintain the intellectual life
of our community and abstract systems of morality
have not conveyed devotion and the power of
obedience with their ideals and imperatives. Idealistic and realistic metaphysics, perfectionist and
hedonistic ethics have been poor substitutes for
the New Testament, and churches which feed on
such nourishment seem subject to spiritual rickets.
Yet it is not the necessity of staying alive which
forces our community to speak in historical terms.
It is not a self-evident truth that the church ought
to live; neither the historical nor the confessional
standpoint can accept self-preservation as the first
law of life, since in history we know that death is
the law of even the best life and in faith we understand that to seek life is to lose it. The church's
compulsion arises out of its need—since it is a living
church—to say truly what it stands for and out of

its inability to do so otherwise than by telling the story of its life.

The preachers and theologians of the modern church must do what New Testament evangelists did because their situation permits no other method. From the point of view of historical beings we can speak only about that which is also in our time and which is seen through the medium of our history. We are in history as the fish is in water and what we mean by the revelation of God can be indicated only as we point through the medium in which we live. When we try other methods we find ourselves still in the old predicament. Since all men are in nature, though their histories vary, we think we may be able to direct them to the God we mean in preaching and worship by pointing as Jesus did to the rain, the sun, the sparrows and the lilies of the field, or to those subtler wonders which microscope and telescope and even more refined instruments of intelligence discover in the common world. As natural rather than historical theologians we try to divorce nature from history and ask men to listen to its praise of the Creator. But such theology is also implicitly historical. Being in Christian history it looks on nature with the mind of Christ, as even Jesus himself, pointing out God's care of beasts and flowers, did so as one whose eyes had been instructed by Moses and the prophets. We cannot point in space to spatial things or in a general time to generally temporal things, saying that what we mean by word of God and by revelation can be known if men will but look together at stars and trees and flowers. It is with Kant in his time-space we must regard the starry heavens, and with Jeremiah see the blossoming almond, and with Jesus behold the lilies of the field before we can read words of God in nature's book. Nature regarded through our history is indeed a symbol of what we mean, a pointer to God; but nature uninterpreted through our history and faith, or torn out of this context and placed in another does not indicate what we mean. It means various things according to the point of view from which it is regarded and the context in which it stands—utter indifference to man and all his works in the context of despair, a blessing upon brutality from the point of view of confidence in military might, and a dominant interest in mathematics in the context of faith in mathematical thought as the only road to truth.

If nature uninterpreted through our history affords us no symbol of what revelation means, Scripture, nature's rival in theology, is in the same position. It may be said that though we are historical beings we can still contemplate from this moving point we occupy a super-historical word of God. So many early Protestants seemed to think in so far as they equated Scriptures with revelation. Yet the Reformers knew—though less vividly it

may be than their successors—that the Scriptures as
a collection of tales and observations about religion
and life, of laws and precepts, as a book containing
moral, political, astronomical and anthropological
ideas, reveals nothing save the state of culture of
the men who wrote its parts or of the groups who
related the legends recorded in later time. We cannot point to Scriptures saying that what we mean
can be known if men will but read what is there
written. We must read the law with the mind of
the prophets and the prophets with the eyes of
Jesus; we must immerse ourselves with Paul in the
story of the crucifixion, and read Paul with the aid
of the spirit in the church if we would find revelation in the Scriptures. A history that was recorded
forwards, as it were, must be read backwards
through our history if it is to be understood as
revelation. Doubtless we are confronted here by an
ancient problem of the church which appears in all
the discussions about law and gospel and about
spirit and letter. Yet it is evident that when the
church speaks of revelation it never means simply
the Scriptures, but only Scriptures read from the
point of view and in the context of church history.
The Scriptures point to God and through Scriptures God points to men when they are read by
those who share the same background which the
community which produced the letter possessed, or
by those who participate in the common life of

which the Scriptures contain the record. Doubtless the Bible differs from nature, being the external form in which our history is preserved and so being indispensable to a community whose history is nowhere recorded in nature, as the history of purely natural communities is. But like nature the Bible can be read in many different contexts and will mean different things accordingly. Translated and read in the nationalistic community it does not point to the Father of Jesus Christ but to blood and soil and tribal deity; read by those whose minds are filled with the history and memories of democratic society it does not point to the intrinsically good God but to the intrinsically valuable individual, and the word that comes through it is a word about liberty from political and economic bondage rather than about liberty from slavery to self and sin. In Protestantism we have long attempted to say what we mean by revelation by pointing to the Scriptures, but we have found that we cannot do so save as we interpret them in a community in which men listen for the word of God in the reading of the Scriptures, or in which men participate in the same spiritual history out of which the record came. The latest movement in New Testament criticism, Form Criticism, underlines this fact for us—that the book arose out of the life of the Church and that we cannot know an historical Jesus save as we look through the history and with the history of the community that loved and worshipped him. A Jesus of history apart from the particular history in which he appears is as unknown and as unknowable as any sense-object apart from the sense-qualities in which it appears to us.

When we have found these ways of circumventing our historical situation and of abandoning our historical point of view obstructed, we may be tempted, with the individualists of all time, to seek a direct path to what we mean through inner religious experience. Can we not say that when we speak of God and revelation we mean events which occur in the privacy of our personal, inner life or what we feel to be basic in our moral consciousness? Yet once more we discover that visions, numinous feelings, sense of reality, knowledge of duty and worth may be interpreted in many ways. We cannot speak of inner light at all, save in ejaculations signifying nothing to other men, unless we define its character in social terms, that is in terms which come out of our history. The "true" seed within, the "right" spirit, can be distinguished from false seeds and evil spirits only by the use of criteria which are not purely individual and biographical. We discriminate between the light within and spiritual will-o'-the-wisps by reference to a "Christ" within. But the word "Christ" comes out of social history and has a meaning not derived from individual experience. Religious experience and moral sense are to be found in many different settings and can be interpreted from many different points of view. The sense of the numinous accompanies many strange acts of worship; it may have been far stronger when human sacrifice was offered to pagan deities than it has ever been in Christianity. High moral devotion and a keen sense of duty point many men today to domestic and tribal gods. What the unconquerable movements of the human heart toward worship and devotion really mean, how their errors may be distinguished from their truths, and how they are to be checked cannot be known save as they are experienced and disciplined in a community with a history. Obedience to moral imperatives, worship and prayer are indispensable and inescapable in the Christian church; they are inseparable from the listening for God's word. But what they mean, what their content must be and to what ends they ought to be directed we cannot understand save as we bring to bear upon them our remembrance of an obedience unto death, of the imperatives which have come to us through history, of the Lord's prayers in the garden and on the mount, and of a worship in a temple whose inner sanctuary was empty. Religious and moral experience are always in some history and in some social setting that derives from the past. They also offer us no way of avoiding the use of our history in saying what we mean.

This necessity is a source of scandal in the Christian church, which is a mystery to itself at this point. To live and think in this way seems to mean that we navigate the oceans and skies of our world by dead reckoning, computing our position from a latitude and longitude determined nineteen hundred years ago, using a log that is in part undecipherable and a compass of conscience notoriously subject to deviation. Objections arise in the crew not only because other vessels claim to possess more scientific apparatus for determining where they are and whither they are going, but because revelation, if it be revelation of God, must offer men something more immovable than the pole star and something more precise than our measurements of the winds and currents of history can afford.

Revelation cannot mean history, we must say to ourselves in the church, if it also means God. What we see from the historical point of view and what we believe in as we occupy that standpoint must be two different things. For surely what is seen in history is not a universal, absolute, independent source and goal of existence, not impartial justice nor infinite mercy, but particularity, finiteness, opinions that pass, caprice, arbitrariness, accident, brutality, wrong on the throne and right on the scaffold. The claims of the evangelists of historical revelation seem wholly inconsistent with their faith. When they speak of a just God they point to a process so unequal that only those born in a special time and space receive faith in him while all who lived before or in cultures with a different history are condemned to ignorance of what they ought to know for the sake of their soul's health and life.

Moreover revelation cannot mean both history and God any more than it can mean both nature and God. The events of history to which Christian revelation refers may be regarded from the scientific, objective, non-committed point of view as well as nature can be. So regarded they have no greater value than other events. They can be studied in their cause-effect relationship, in their cultural, geographic, economic and political contexts; when this is done it is apparent that the scientist has as little need for the hypothesis of divine action as Laplace had in his astronomy. The birth of Jesus and the legends about it, the Sermon on the Mount, the miracles and parables, the crucifixion and resurrection stories, the institution of the sacraments—all these may be explained by noting their place in a series of other events in Jewish and Hellenistic history or in the development of religious, philosophical, political and economic movements. At best such historic description will make use of the category of individuality, pointing out the uniqueness of each event and the particular way in which general principles are made concrete in it. But such uniqueness is a characteristic of all events in time and the unique Jesus does not differ in this respect from the unique Socrates and the unique Hitler. Objective history cannot, without denying its method and its point of view, require a consideration for the life of Jesus differing from that which it brings to bear on other individual events. It can only record another unique fact—that the church and Western culture have attached great religious significance to Jesus. It may seek further to account for this new individual event by reference to some general tendencies in human nature and to their unique manifestations in the first and later centuries of the Christian era.

So it appears that if revelation means history it cannot also mean the object of faith, save in this purely factual and wholly opaque sense that certain people have attached transcendent value to certain events.

The problem presents itself to the Christian church in a third way. If revelation means history, is not faith in revelation identical with belief in the occurrence of certain past, divine events and is not such an identification an actual denial of faith in a living God? Concentration on history in the church has led to repeated revolts by men of piety and good will for whom God was not a "then and there" but a "here and now" and for whom faith was not belief in the actuality of historical events but confidence in an abiding, ruling will of love. Trusting in

God now, seeking to obey his present commandments, struggling with contemporary evil, such men have rebelled against the equation of historical belief with Christian faith and against the identification of present moral commandments with precepts given to Jews or to Pauline churches in ancient times. They have refused to make the forgiveness of sin a juridical act of the past rather than a contemporary experience; they have insisted on the present reality of the Holy Spirit as more important to Christians than a Pentecostal miracle in the early church. Such vital faith, seeking contact with a present Lord and Giver of Life, must always revolt against historic antiquarianism even as it must reject a futurism for which God, forgiveness and moral obedience are only future possibilities without present validity.

Revelation in history involves other difficulties. Questions about predestination and freedom, eternity and time, progress and decline, and many others of like sort assail the mind of the Christian in his dilemma of historic faith. Though he concedes the fact that he must speak as an historic being and also that the church has always thought in historical terms, he is puzzled by the relation of faith and history. History seems always to lead to doubt rather than to faith.

In the bewilderment which assails him in this situation the modern Christian, like many a predecessor in the church, is tempted again and again to drop the history and to hold fast to the faith, to give up the Jesus of history while affirming afresh his loyalty to the Christ of faith. But faith is a strange thing; it is not sufficient to itself and will not work alone. It is like the eye which cannot perceive the depth and distance and solidity of things save as it has a partner. Or it is like Adam who seeks a helpmeet among all the creatures and cannot be fruitful in loins or mind until an Eve is given him for conversation. And Christian faith, having tried many other partners, has found that these can speak with it of its God only if they have been schooled in Christian history. Nor are there any among them that speak a universal language; if they do not speak in Galilean accents some other province not less small in the infinite world has shaped their voices and minds in its own way. Philosophy, as historical in all its forms as religion, can indeed share and strengthen the life of faith, but only when it speaks out of a mind that has been filled with Jewish and Christian memories. The church is not ill at ease with Descartes, Spinoza, Locke, Berkeley and Kant; but then the God of whom these philosophers write is always something more than their conceptual systems have defined. As Professors Gilson and A. E. Taylor have again reminded us recently, the God of modern philosophers is more than the God of their philosophies; he could not mean so much in their thought if he did not mean more than their thought about him expresses. He is always the God of history, of Abraham, Isaac and Jacob, or the Father of Jesus Christ and not only the God of abstract thought.

It remains true that Christian faith cannot escape from partnership with history, however many other partners it may choose. With this it has been mated and to this its loyalty belongs; the union is as indestructible as that of reason and sense experience in the natural sciences. But though this is true the question remains, how can it be true? How can revelation mean both history and God?

II. *History as Lived and as Seen*

We may be helped toward a solution of the problem of history and faith by reflection upon the fact that the history to which we point when we speak of revelation is not the succession of events which an uninterested spectator can see from the outside but our own history. It is one thing to perceive from a safe distance the occurrences in a stranger's life and quite a different thing to ponder the path of one's own destiny, to deal with the why and whence and whither of one's own existence. Of a man who has been blind and who has come to see, two histories can be written. A scientific case history will describe what happened to his optic nerve or to the crystalline lens, what technique the surgeon used or by what medicines a physician wrought the cure, through what stages of recovery the patient passed. An autobiography, on the other hand, may barely mention these things but it will tell what happened to a self that had lived in darkness and now saw again trees and the sunrise, children's faces and the eyes of a friend. Which of these histories can be a parable of revelation, the outer history or the inner one, the story of what happened to the cells of a body or the story of what happened to a self? When we speak of revelation in the Christian church we refer to *our* history, to the history of selves or to history as it is lived and apprehended from within.

The distinction between *our* history and events in impersonal time, or between history as lived and as contemplated from the outside may be illustrated by contrasting parallel descriptions of the same social event. Lincoln's Gettysburg Address begins with history: "Four-score and seven years ago our fathers brought forth upon this continent a new nation, conceived in liberty and dedicated to the proposition that all men are created free and equal." The same event is described in the *Cambridge Modern History* in the following fashion: "On July 4, 1776, Congress passed the resolution which made the colonies independent communities, issuing at the same time the well-known Declaration of Independence. If we regard the Declaration as the assertion of an abstract political theory, criticism and condemnation are easy. It sets out with a general proposition so vague as to be practically useless. The doctrine of the equality of men, unless it be qualified and conditioned by reference to special circumstance, is either a barren truism or a delusion."

The striking dissimilarity between these two accounts may be explained as being due merely to a difference of sentiment; the blind devotion of the patriot is opposed to the critical acumen and dispassionate judgment of the scientific historian. But the disparity goes deeper. The difference in sentiment is so profound because the beings about which the accounts speak differ greatly; the "Congress" is one thing, "our fathers" are almost another reality. The proposition that all men are created free and equal, to which the fathers dedicated their lives, their fortunes and their sacred honor, and which for their children is to be the object of a new devotion, seems to belong to a different order of ideas than that to which the vague and useless, barren truism or delusion belongs. Though these various terms point to the same ultimate realities the latter are seen in different aspects and apprehended in different contexts. Moreover it seems evident that the terms the external historian employs are not more truly descriptive of the things-in-themselves than those the statesman uses and that the former's understanding

of what really happened is not more accurate than
the latter's. In the one case the events of history are
seen from the outside, in the other from the inside.
Lincoln spoke of what had happened in *our* history,
of what had made and formed us and to which
we remain committed so long as we continue to
exist as Americans; he spoke of purposes which lie
in our enduring past and are therefore the purposes
of our present life; he described the history of living
beings and not data relating to dead things. It is a
critical history but the criticism of its author is not
directed toward the general propositions so much
as to the human beings who measure themselves and
are measured by means of those general propositions; criticism is moral, directed toward selves and
their community. The other account abstracts from
living selves with their resolutions and commit-
ments, their hopes, and fears. It is not critical of
men but of things; documents and propositions are
its objects. The events it describes happened in impersonal time and are recorded less in the memories
of persons than in books and monuments.

The example from American history may be
duplicated in the history of every other community.
Pericles' Funeral Oration appeals to memory and
may be paralleled by many an external account of
the rise of an empire "acquired by men who knew
their duty . . . and who if they ever failed in an
enterprise would not allow their virtues to be lost

to their country, but freely gave their lives to her as the fairest offering they could present at her feast." Hosea's account of the childhood of Israel and the Psalmist's recall of what "we have heard and known and our fathers have told us" have their counterparts in ethnological descriptions of early Semitic tribal life. Shakespeare's invocations of memories clustering about "this royal throne of kings, this sceptred isle . . . this land of such dear souls, this dear, dear land," and Burke's reverential regard for a tradition in which the hand of God is visible may be matched by cool, aloof accounts of the rise of British empire. The distinctions between the two types of history cannot be made by applying the value-judgment of true and false but must be made by reference to differences of perspective. There are true and false appeals to memory as well as true and false external descriptions but only uncritical dogmatism will affirm that truth is the prerogative of one of the points of view. Events may be regarded from the outside by a non-participating observer; then they belong to the history of things. They may be apprehended from within, as items in the destiny of persons and communities; then they belong to a life-time and must be interpreted in a context of persons with their resolutions and devotions.

The differences between the outer history of things and the inner history of selves which appear in these illustrations need to be analyzed in a little more detail in preparation for our effort to understand the relation of revelation to history. It appears, first of all, that the data of external history are all impersonal; they are ideas, interests, movements among things. Even when such history deals with human individuals it seeks to reduce them to impersonal parts. Jesus becomes, from this point of view, a complex of ideas about ethics and eschatology, of psychological and biological elements. Other persons are dealt with in the same manner. One may look for an efficient factor among such impersonal elements, though its determination involves the peril of forsaking the objective point of view, as when a Marxist historian chooses economic elements or an intellectualist regards ideas in the mind as the motivating forces in history. Internal history, on the other hand, is not a story of things in juxtaposition or succession; it is personal in character. Here the final data are not elusive atoms of matter or thought but equally elusive selves. In such history it is not the idea of the soul which Socrates thought and communicated that is important but rather the soul of Socrates, "all glorious within," the soul of the "most righteous man of the whole age." In external history we deal with objects; in internal history our concern is with subjects. In the former, to use Professor Alexander's distinction, our data are "-eds," what is believed, sensed, conceived; but in the latter what is given is always an "-ing," a knowing, a willing, a believing, a feeling. Or, as Martin Buber would put it, in external history all relations are between an "I" and an "it," while in the other they are relations between "I" and "Thou"; moreover the "I" in the "I-it" relation differs from the self in the "I-Thou" setting.

Speaking as critical idealists we might say that in external history all apprehension and interpretation of events must employ the category of individuality but in internal history it is the category of personality that must be used in perceiving and understanding whatever happens. In *our* history all events occur not to impersonal bodies but to selves in community with other selves and they must be so understood. After the fashion of critical idealism we may distinguish external history as a realm of the pure reason from internal history as a sphere of the pure practical reason, though it is evident that Kantian reason must be understood in far more historical fashion than was the case in the eighteenth century when neither pure nor practical reason were thought to be socially and historically conditioned.

We may employ the method of critical realism rather than of critical idealism in making our distinction between external and internal history. From the realistic point of view we are concerned in external history to abstract from all that is merely secondary, from subjective and partisan accounts of what happened; we seek to set forth the primary characteristics of each event as these may be defined by taking into account the reports of eye-witnesses, of contemporary documents and those "permanent possibilities of sensation," the enduring institutions, the constant movements of mind and will available to the experience of all percipients. In internal history on the other hand we are not concerned with the primary and secondary elements of external historical perception but with "tertiary qualities," with values. These are not private and evanescent as the secondary elements are but common and verifiable in a community of selves; yet they are not objective in the sense in which the primary qualities of external perception are said to be objective. Critical realism, however, like critical idealism, is so strongly conditioned by its historic association with non-historically minded natural science and particularly with mathematics that its use in this realm of thinking about history requires a prior readjustment of all its concepts. It is enough to point out that the distinctions which appear in all critical philosophy as between knowledge of the external world and knowledge of the internal, which drive even the most dogmatic positivists to assert that ethics and religion belong to some other realm than that with which objective knowledge is concerned, must also be made in our understanding of history. There is a descriptive and there is a normative knowledge of history and neither type is reducible to the terms of the other.

The distinction may be made clearer by noting the differences in the conceptions of value, time and human association which are employed in the two contexts.

In external history value means valency or strength. The objective historian must measure the importance of an event or factor by the effect it has on other events or factors in the series. Though he is also a self, living in community, having a destiny, and so unable wholly to escape a moral point of view, as scientific historian he is bound to suppress his own value-judgments as much as possible. Not what is noblest in his sight but what is most effective needs to be treated most fully. So Alexander may have a larger place in his account than Socrates, though as a self the historian may elect to follow right to martyrdom rather than might to victory. Economic motives in the framing of the American Constitution may require far more attention than moral ideals, though the historian be one who has abjured the ownership of property for himself and may live a semi-monastic life. Looking upon events in the manner of an impartial spectator, he seeks to suppress every response of love or repugnance and to apply a more or less quantitative measure of strength in determining the importance of persons or events.

In internal history, however, value means worth for selves; whatever cannot be so valued is unimportant and may be dropped from memory. Here the death of Socrates, the birth of Lincoln, Peter's martyrdom, Luther's reform, Wesley's conversion, the landing of the Pilgrims, the granting of Magna Charta are events to be celebrated; this history calls for joy and sorrow, for days of rededication and of shriving, for tragic participation and for jubilees. The valuable here is that which bears on the destiny of selves; not what is strongest is most important but what is most relevant to the lives of "I's" and "Thou's." Value here means quality, not power; but the quality of valued things is one which only selves can apprehend. In this context we do not measure the worth of even our own desires by their strength but by their relevance to the destiny of the self.

As with value so with time. In our internal history time has a different feel and quality from that of the external time with which we deal as exoteric historians. The latter time resembles that of physics. Physics knows a plain man's time which has for him a valency like that of the "real" money of his province; it also knows a sophisticated time which is aware of its own relativity. So in external history there is the time of the naïve chronicler with his acceptance of dynastic dates, his reckonings of years since creation, his A. D.'s and B. C.'s; or this history may think of time in the sophisticated way of a culture philosophy. But all these time-conceptions have one thing in common—they are all quantitative; all these times are numbered. Such time is always serial. In the series, past events are gone and future happenings are not yet. In internal history, on the other hand, our time is our duration. What is past is not gone; it abides in us as our memory; what is future is not non-existent but present in us as our potentiality. Time here is organic or it is social, so that past and future associate with each other in the present. Time in our history is not another dimension of the external space world in which we live, but a dimension of our life and of our community's being. We are not in this time but it is in us. It is not associated with space in a unity of space-time but it is inseparable from life in the continuity of life-time. We do not speak of it in precise numbers but say in poetic fashion with Lincoln, "four-score and seven years ago," meaning not eighty-seven but our remembered past. In humbler fashion we correlate, as gossips do, the lives and deaths and wars of kings with shocks and joys in our own history. Such time is not a number but a living, a stream of consciousness, a flow of feeling, thought and will. It is not measurable by the hours and years of a planetary and solar rhythm;

its ebb and flow, its pulsations and surges, its births and deaths and resurrections are incommensurable with lunar or atomic tides. If they are to be measured it must be done by a comparison with other inner alternations; in our history we do not correlate the death of the heart with the declining sun nor its rebirth with nature's spring but with a crucifixion of the son of God and with his rising to new life.

Human association also differs when regarded from the external or internal points of view. The external knower must see societies as made up of atomic individuals related to each other by external bonds. Yet even the human individuals are depersonalized, since they are understood as complexes of psychological and biological factors. Society, to his view, is a vast and intricate organization of interests, drives or instincts, beliefs, customs, laws, constitutions, inventions, geographic and climatic data, in which a critical and diligent inquiry can discover some intelligible structures and moving patterns of relation. In internal history, on the other hand, society is a community of selves. Here we do not only live among other selves but they live in us and we in them. Relations here are not external but internal so that we are our relations and cannot be selves save as we are members of each other. When there is strife in this community there is strife and pain in us and when it is at peace we have peace in ourselves. Here social memory is not what is written in books and preserved in libraries, but what—not without the mediation of books and monuments, to be sure—is our own past, living in every self. When we become members of such a community of selves we adopt its past as our own and thereby are changed in our present existence. So immigrants and their children do, for whom Pilgrims become true fathers and the men of the Revolution their own liberators; so we do in the Christian community when the prophets of the Hebrews become our prophets and the Lord of the early disciples is acknowledged as our Lord. Not what is after the flesh—that is what is externally seen—but what is after the spirit—what has become a part of our own lives as selves—is the important thing in this internal view. In our history association means community, the participation of each living self in a common memory and common hope no less than in a common world of nature.

It may be said that to speak of history in this fashion is to try to think with poets rather than with scientists. That is what we mean, for poets think of persons, purposes and destinies. It is just their Jobs and Hamlets that are not dreamt of in philosophies which rule out from the company of true being whatever cannot be numbered or included in an impersonal pattern. Drama and epic set forth pattern too, but it is one of personal relations. Hence we may call internal history dramatic and its truth dramatic truth, though drama in this case does not mean fiction.

The relevance of this distinction between two histories to the subject of revelation must now have become apparent. When the evangelists of the New Testament and their successors pointed to history as the starting point of their faith and of their understanding of the world it was internal history that they indicated. They did not speak of events, as impersonally apprehended, but rather of what had happened to them in their community. They recalled the critical point in their own life-time when they became aware of themselves in a new way as they came to know the self on whom they were dependent. They turned to a past which was not gone but which endured in them as their memory, making them what they were. So for the later church, history was always the story of "our fathers," of "our Lord," and of the actions of "our God."

The inspiration of Christianity has been derived from history, it is true, but not from history as seen by a spectator; the constant reference is to subjective events, that is to events in the lives of subjects. What distinguishes such historic recall from the private histories of mystics is that it refers to communal events, remembered by a community and in a community. Subjectivity here is not equivalent to isolation, non-verifiability and ineffability; our history can be communicated and persons can refresh as well as criticize each other's memories of what has happened to them in the common life; on the basis of a common past they can think together about the common future.

Such history, to be sure, can only be confessed by the community, and in this sense it is esoteric. One cannot point to historic events in the lives of selves as though they were visible to any external point of view. Isaiah cannot say that in the year King Uzziah died God became visible in the temple nor Paul affirm that Jesus the Lord appears to travellers on the Damascus road. Neither will any concentration of attention on Isaiah and Paul, any detailed understanding of their historical situation, enable the observer to see what they saw. One must look with them and not at them to verify their visions, participate in their history rather than regard it if one would apprehend what they apprehended. The history of the inner life can only be confessed by selves who speak of what happened to them in the community of other selves.

III. *Faith in Our History*

The distinction between history as known by the pure and as apprehended by the practical reason, though it raises difficulties that must be met, does assist us to understand how it is possible for the word "revelation" to point to history and yet point to God also. It cannot point to God, as we have noted, if the history to which it directs attention is the chain of events that an impersonal eye or mind apprehends. For such history, abstracting from human selves, must also abstract events from the divine self and, furthermore, while it may furnish motives for belief in the occurrence of certain happenings it does not invite trust in a living God.

The error frequently made in the Christian community which has been the occasion for the rise of many difficulties in understanding and propagating the historical faith has been the location of revelation in external history or in history as known from the non-participating point of view. So revelation has been identified with some miracle, whether this was the single act of a person or his whole life or the life of a community, such as Israel or the church. In this way certain events in external history were set apart as sacred, or a sacred history of one community has been opposed to the secular histories of other societies. Sacred events were inserted into a context otherwise secular and the continuity between the two types of events denied. It was denied that the events of holy history were subject to the same type of explanation which might be offered for secular happenings; that so-called secular events might have a sacred meaning for those who participated in them as selves was not thought possible.

Much so-called orthodoxy identified revelation with Scriptures and regarded the latter as wholly miraculous, the product of an inspiration which suspended the ordinary processes of human thought and guaranteed inerrancy. But to validate the Scriptural miracle another needed to be inserted into history since that which stands completely alone is an impenetrable mystery, no matter how much astonishment it calls forth. So miraculous Scriptures were related to miracles in the realm of nature, to a sun that stood still, a virgin-born child, to water turned by a word into wine. Furthermore the psychological miracle of prophecy as a supernatural foretelling of events, as though by second-sight, was introduced to validate the wonder of the Bible. The consequence of this method of argument was that two systems of reality on the same plane—a natural, historical, rational system and a supernatural, super-historical and super-rational system— were set beside each other. They were on the same plane, perceived by the same organs of sense and apprehended by the same minds, yet there was no real relation between them. Revelation took place within the supernatural and super-historical system; reason operated in the natural series of events. The distinction between the history in which revelation occurred and that in which there was no revelation was transferred to persons and things having history; there were natural and unnatural events, persons and groups. It was assumed that the differences between nature and super-nature were due not to the beholder's situation but to the things viewed while the point of view remained constant. Hence arose the conflict between history and faith. For sacred events in a secular context must be secularly apprehended and to demand of men that they should exempt certain events in the chain of perceived happenings from the application of the laws or principles with which they apprehend the others is to ask the impossible or to make everything unintelligible. How much the tendency to self-defensiveness and self-glorification in Christianity contributed to this effort to exempt the faith and its history from the judgments applicable to ordinary events it is not possible to say. But it must be noted that the consequence of the attempt to isolate sacred from secular history led not only to fruitless quarrels with natural and social science but also to internal conflict and inconsistency since it tended to substitute belief in the occurrence of miraculous events for faith in God and invited dispute about the relative importance of many wonders.

If the distinction between history as seen from without by a pure reason and from within by a practical reason, and if the denial of the exclusive validity of either view be allowed, we are enabled to understand not only how faith and history may be associated but how in the nature of the case they must be allied. An inner history, life's flow as regarded from the point of view of living selves, is always an affair of faith. As long as a man lives he must believe in something for the sake of which he lives; without belief in something that makes life worth living man cannot exist. If, as Tolstoi points out in his *Confession*, man does not see the temporality and futility of the finite he will believe in the finite as worth living for; if he can no longer have faith in the value of the finite he will believe in the infinite or else die. Man as a practical, living being never exists without a god or gods; some things there are to which he must cling as the sources and goals of his activity, the centers of value. As a rule men are polytheists, referring now to this and now to that valued being as the source of life's meaning. Sometimes they live for Jesus' God, sometimes for country and sometimes for Yale. For the most part they make gods out of themselves or out of the work of their own hands, living for their own glory as persons and as communities. In any case the faith that life is worth living and the definite reference of life's meaning to specific beings or values is as inescapable a part of human existence as the activity of reason. It is no less true that man is a believing animal in this sense than that he is a rational animal. Without such faith men might exist, but not as selves. Being selves they as surely have something for which to live as selves as being rational they have objects to understand.

Such faith in gods or in values for which men live is inseparable from internal history. It is the gods that give unity to the events of personal life. A nation has an internal history so far as its members have some common center of reference, some good for which they live together, whether that be an abstract value, such as equality or democracy which unites them in common devotion, or whether it be the personalized community itself, such as Athena, or Britannia, or Columbia. A man has one internal history so far as he is devoted to one value. For the most part persons and communities do not have a single internal history because their faiths are various and the events of life cannot be related to one continuing and abiding good. They have "too many selves to know the one," too many histories, too many gods; alongside their published and professed history there are suppressed but true stories of inner life concentrated about gods of whom they are ashamed. Without a single faith there is no real unity of the self or of a community, therefore no unified inner history but only a multiplicity of memories and destinies. Inner history and inner faith belong together, as the existence of self and an object of devotion for the sake of which the self lives are inseparable.

The relation is something like that of animal faith in the existence of an external world and the data of experience. By an unconquerable compulsion, given with life itself, we believe in the reality of the trees we see, the ground we walk upon, the tables, chairs and houses we touch and use, the food and drink we taste. We count upon enduring realities and are not usually put to shame. No matter how refined our scepticism grows, how far into infinity we pursue the constituent elements of our objects, how ethereal to the mind's eye the natural world becomes, we rely upon the enduring stuff of our environment and we continue to be nourished and to be borne up. "Nature," that is to say human nature, is sufficient to dispel the clouds of scepticism, as Hume himself pointed out. Without this animal faith in a dependable external world we literally would not live as bodies, for if we were true sceptics we would be errant fools to eat food made up of sense-data only, to breathe an unsubstantial air with unreal lungs, to walk with unreal feet upon a non-existent earth toward imaginary goals. By faith, by counting upon persistent factors in our environment we live as bodies and with our brains think out this common world. But what the factors are on which we can count, what the permanent possibilities of sensation are on which we can depend in thought and act, that we cannot know save through repeated and common experience. The necessity of an animal faith in objective reality may be prior to all experience but concrete faith in any particular element in our world as dependable does not exist save as it is made possible by sense-experience. Faith is inseparably connected with experience; but neither faith nor sense-experience can be substitutes for each other. So also the faith of selves in a source of value or in a god is inseparable from the inner experience of selves, from what happens to them in their history. They cannot but believe that these events, the joys and sorrows of the self, have meaning but what the meaning is cannot be known apart from inner history. The necessity of believing in a god is given with the life of selves, but what gods are dependable, which of them can be counted on day after day and which are idols—products of erroneous imagination—cannot be known save through the experiences of inner history.

The standpoint of faith, of a self directed toward gods or God, and the standpoint of practical reason, of a self with values and with a destiny, are not incompatible; they are probably identical. To be a self is to have a god; to have a god is to have history, that is, events connected in a meaningful pattern; to have one god is to have one history. God and the history of selves in community belong together in inseparable union.

IV. *Relations of Internal and External History*

Though we may be persuaded that there is a valid distinction between history as lived and history as observed by the external spectator; though we may recognize a relative validity in either type while noting the close relation of faith and the life of selves to the practical knowledge of our destiny; yet questions about the relations of the two types of history are bound to arise in our minds. When we have understood that revelation must be looked for in the events that have happened to us, which live in our memory, we cannot refrain from asking ourselves how this history is related to the external accounts of our life. To such questions we must give some attention before we can proceed to a closer definition of the meaning of revelation.

The two-aspect theory of history, like the two-aspect theory of body and mind, may be made necessary by the recognition that all knowing is conditioned by the point of view, that the exaltation of differences of understanding into differences of being raises more problems than it solves, that the intimate relations of subjective and objective truth require the rejection of every extreme dualism. But it is evident that the theory does not solve the problem of unity in duality and duality in unity. It only states the paradox in a new form and every paradox is the statement of a dilemma rather than an escape from it. It is important, of course, that a paradox be correctly stated and that false simplicity be avoided. We have made some advance toward a correct statement of our dilemma, we believe, when we have recognized that the duality of the history in which there is revelation and of the history in which there is none, is not the duality of different groups or communities, or when we have understood that this dualism runs right through Christian history itself. We are enabled to see why we can speak of revelation only in connection with our own history without affirming or denying its reality in the history of other communities into whose inner life we cannot penetrate without abandoning ourselves and our community. The two-aspect theory allows us to understand how revelation can be in history and yet not be identifiable with miraculous events as visible to an external observer and how events that are revelatory in our history, sources of unconquerable certainty for us, can yet be analyzed in profane fashion by the observer. But the paradox remains. It is but another form of the two-world thinking in which Christianity is forever involved and we need not expect that in thinking about history we shall be able to escape the dilemma that confronts our faith in every other sphere. One-world thinking, whether as this-worldliness or as other-worldliness, has always betrayed Christianity into the denial of some of its fundamental convictions.

It will do so in the case of history no less than in
metaphysics and ethics. But how to think in two-
worldly terms without lapsing into di-theism remains a problem of great import for faith.

There is no speculative escape from the dilemma,
that is to say we cannot absorb internal history
into external history nor yet transcend both practical and objective points of view in such a way as
to gain a knowledge of history superior to both and
able to unite them into a new whole. If we begin
with the spectator's knowledge of events we cannot proceed to the participant's apprehension.
There is no continuous movement from an objective inquiry into the life of Jesus to a knowledge of
him as the Christ who is our Lord. Only a decision
of the self, a leap of faith, a *metanoia* or revolution
of the mind can lead from observation to participation and from observed to lived history. And this
is true of all other events in sacred history.

It may be thought that the problem of the relation of inner and outer history can be solved by a
determination of what the events, visible in two
aspects, really are in themselves. But the idea of
events-in-themselves like that of things-in-themselves is an exceedingly difficult one. The ultimate
nature of an event is not what it is in its isolation
only but what it is in its connection with all other
events, not what it is for itself but also what it is
from an inclusive point of view. The event, as it

really is, is the event as it is for God who knows it at the same time and in one act from within as well as from without, in its isolation as well as in its community with all other events. Such knowledge of the nature of events is beyond the possibility of the finite point of view. Being finite souls with finite minds in finite bodies men are confined to a double and partial knowledge which is yet not knowledge of double reality.

Though there be no metaphysical or meta-historical solution of the problem of historical dualism there is a practical solution. Though we cannot speak of the way in which the two aspects of historical events are ultimately related in the event-for-God we can describe their functional relationship for us. Such a description must once more be given confessionally, not as a statement of what all men ought to do but as statement of what we have found it necessary to do in the Christian community on the basis of the faith which is our starting point.

In the first place, beginning with internal knowledge of the destiny of self and community, we have found it necessary in the Christian church to accept the external views of ourselves which others have set forth and to make these external histories events of spiritual significance. To see ourselves as others see us, or to have others communicate to us what they see when they regard our lives from the outside is to have a moral experience. Every external history of ourselves, communicated to us, becomes an event in inner history. So the outside view of democracy offered by Marxists has become an event in the inner history of democracy. It has responded to that external view with defense but also with self-criticism and reformation. External histories of Christianity have become important events in its inner history. Celsus' description of the sources of Christian belief and his criticism of miraculous super-naturalism, Gibbon's, Feuerbach's and Kautsky's accounts of Christianity, other surveys made from the points of view of idealistic or positivistic philosophy, of Judaism or of the history of religion —these have all been events in the internal history of Christianity. The church has had to respond to them. Though it knew that such stories were not *the* truth about it, it willingly or unwillingly, sooner or later, recognized *a* truth about it in each one. In so far as it apprehended these events in its history, these descriptions and criticisms of itself, with the aid of faith in the God of Jesus Christ it discerned God's judgment in them and made them occasions for active repentance. Such external histories have helped to keep the church from exalting itself as though its inner life rather than the God of that inner life were the center of its attention and the ground of its faith. They have reminded the church of the earthen nature of the vessel in which the treasure of faith existed. In this practical way external history has not been incompatible with inner life but directly contributory to it.

Secondly, just because the Christian community remembers the revelatory moment in its own history it is required to regard all events, even though it can see most of them only from an external point of view, as workings of the God who reveals himself and so to trace with piety and disinterestedness, so far as its own fate is concerned, the ways of God in the lives of men. It is necessary for the Christian community, living in faith, to look upon all the events of time and to try to find in them the workings of one mind and will. This is necessary because the God who is found in inner history, or rather who reveals himself there, is not the spiritual life but universal God, the creator not only of the events through which he discloses himself but also of all other happenings. The standpoint of the Christian community is limited, being in history, faith and sin. But what is seen from this standpoint is unlimited. Faith cannot get to God save through historic experience as reason cannot get to nature save through sense-experience. But as reason, having learned through limited experience an intelligible pattern of reality, can seek the evidence of a like pattern in all other experience, so faith having apprehended the divine self in its own history, can and must look for the manifestation of the same self in all other events. Thus prophets, for whom the revelation of God was connected with his mighty acts in the deliverance of Israel from bondage, found the marks of that God's working in the histories of all the nations. The Christian community must turn in like manner from the revelation of the universal God in a limited history to the recognition of his rule and providence in all events of all times and communities. Such histories must be regarded from the outside to be sure; in events so regarded the meeting of human and divine selves cannot be recorded, but all the secondary causes, all the factors of political and social life can be approached with the firm conviction of an underlying unity due to the pervasive presence of the one divine self. It is not possible to describe external history by reference to miraculous deeds but the revelation of the one God makes it possible and necessary to approach the multiplicity of events in all times with the confidence that unity may be found, however hard the quest for it. Where faith is directed to many gods only pluralistic and unconnected histories can be written, if indeed there is any impulsion to understand or write history. Where, through a particular set of historical experiences, the conviction has been established that all events have one source and goal it becomes possible to seek out the uniformities, the dependable patterns of process. That such history, though a product of piety, is not pious history, designed to exalt the inner life of the religious community or to emphasize the importance of religious factors in social life, must be evident. A faithful external history is not interested in faith but in the ways of God, and the more faithful it is the less it may need to mention his name or refer to the revelation in which he was first apprehended, or rather in which he first apprehended the believer. In this sense an external history finds its starting point or impulsion in an internal history.

Not only is the external history of other selves and communities a necessary and possible work of faith on the part of Christians but an external history of itself is its inescapable duty for two reasons. The revelation of God in history is, as we shall see, the revelation of a self. To know God is to be known of him, and therefore also to know the self as it is reflected in God. The church's external history of itself may be described as an effort to see itself with the eyes of God. The simultaneous, unified knowledge from within and from without that we may ascribe to God is indeed impossible to men, but what is simultaneous in his case can in a measure be successive for us. The church cannot attain an inclusive, universal point of view but it can attempt to see the reflection of itself in the eyes of God. What it sees in that reflection is finite, created, limited, corporeal being, alike in every respect to all the other beings of creations. To describe that vision in detail, to see the limited, human character of its founder, the connections between itself and a Judaism to which it often, in false pride, feels superior, between its sacraments and mystery faiths, between Catholicism and feudalism, Protestantism and capitalism, to know itself as the chief of sinners and the most mortal of societies—all this is required of it by a revelation that has come to it through its history.

Moreover, though there is no transition from external observation to internal participation save by decision and faith, yet it is also true that the internal life does not exist without external embodiment. The memory which we know within ourselves as pure activity must have some static aspect which an objective science, we may believe, will in time discover in the very structure of the neural system. What the neural system is to the memory of an individual self that books and monuments are to a common memory. Without the Bible and the rites of the institutional church the inner history of the Christian community could not continue, however impossible it is to identify the memory of that community with the documents. Though we cannot point to what we mean by revelation by directing attention to the historic facts as embodied and as regarded from without, we can have no continuing inner history through which to point without embodiment. "Words without thoughts never to heaven go" but thoughts without words never remain on earth. Moreover such is the alternation of our life that the thought which becomes a word can become thought again only through the mediation of the word; the word which becomes flesh can become word for us again only through the flesh. External history is the medium in which internal history exists and comes to life. Hence knowledge of its external history remains a duty of the church.

In all this we have only repeated the paradox of Chalcedonian Christology and of the two-world ethics of Christianity. But it is necessary to repeat it in our time, especially in view of the all too simple definitions of history and revelation that fail to take account of the duality in union which is the nature of Christian life and history.

We have not yet succeeded in saying what we mean by revelation but have indicated the sphere in which revelation is to be found. That sphere is internal history, the story of what happened to us, the living memory of the community. Our further efforts must be directed to a somewhat more precise determination of the area in which the revelatory event is to be found.

CHAPTER III

REASONS OF THE HEART

I. *Imagination and Reason*

WHEN Christians speak of revelation they point to history not as this can be known by external observers but as it is remembered by participating selves. Yet revelation does not simply mean inner history as a whole nor any arbitrarily chosen part of it.

There are many obscure elements in remembered history which are neither intelligible in themselves nor illuminative of other elements. Among these none are more obscure than the fateful facts of personal and communal self-conscious existence. We do not know why we are ourselves in our particular time and place. Though from an external point of view explanations can be offered which account for the physical conditions of personal and social life, these give no answer to the questions about the origin, the meaning and the destiny of the self. The question why I am I, in this here and now, conditioned by and dependent on this body, and the equally difficult questions communities must raise about themselves indicate obscurities which reveal nothing. They must be illuminated themselves if there is to be anything that can be called revelation.

Our evil deeds are also obscure though they are well-remembered parts of our history as selves. Peter's denials and Judas' betrayal, together with a long succession of like events, are in the story of the Christian community as much as conversions and transfigurations are. These also are neither self-explanatory nor by themselves helpful toward the understanding of other experiences. This is true of pain endured as well as of suffering inflicted on others by our fault. There is no mystery of evil in history or nature regarded from without; in fact no evil of any sort is visible to the spectator who sees only impersonal necessity reigning among things. From the objective point of view betrayals and denials, pains and sufferings are merely facts; they occur without the participation of selves, call for no explanation differing in kind from explanations of other natural facts; they are as worthy of attention and as significant as the heroisms and loyalties of men. Events can be evil only as they occur in the history of selves, as they are related to persons who cause them or who suffer their effects. But the why and wherefore of evil in this context is a mystery and not a revelation.

Further, we may remember in our past some moments of intense feeling when the sense of the numinous was strong, when majestic and awe-inspiring experience called forth strange emotions. But the emotion by itself revealed nothing and later experience often indicated that it was an inadequate response to the situation, perhaps no more than a sense of frustration. It is not to any of these obscurities in our inner history that we point when we speak of revelation.

Revelation means for us that part of our inner history which illuminates the rest of it and which is itself intelligible. Sometimes when we read a difficult book, seeking to follow a complicated argument, we come across a luminous sentence from which we can go forward and backward and so attain some understanding of the whole. Revelation is like that. In his *Religion in the Making* Professor Whitehead has written such illuminating sentences and one of them is this: "Rational religion appeals to the direct intuition of special occasions, and to the elucidatory power of its concepts for all occasions." The special occasion to which we appeal in the Christian church is called Jesus Christ, in whom we see the righteousness of God, his power and wisdom. But from that special occasion we also derive the concepts which make possible the elucidation of all the events in our history. Revelation means this intelligible event which makes all other events intelligible.

Such a revelation, rather than being contrary to reason in our life, is the discovery of rational pattern in it. Revelation means the point at which we can begin to think and act as members of an intelligible and intelligent world of persons. The pattern, to be sure, is discovered in our personal and communal history; it is applicable to events as these are known by participating selves and never primarily or directly applicable to events as seen by non-participants. The obscurities which it explains are not those which bother us as observers of life but those which distress moral agents and sufferers. To use Pascal's phrase here, it is the heart and not the head which finds its reason in revelation. This does not mean that the reason of the heart is in conflict with the reason of the head or that the relations between the two are not very close. It does mean that the reason which is correlate with revelation is practical reason, or the reason of a self rather than of impersonal mind; it implies that the conflict of practical reason is with practical irrationality as pure reason is at war with irrationality in the head and not with reason in the heart. When we use revelation as the basis of our reasoning we seek to conquer the evil imaginations of the heart and not the adequate images of an observing mind.

Reflection on the relations of reason and imagination may assist us at this point in understanding how revelation is a rational principle, so that when we speak of it we point to that occasion in our history which enables us to understand. We make a false distinction when we so separate reason and imagination as to make the former the arbiter in our knowledge of the external world while we regard the inner life as the sphere of the latter. Under the influence of this distinction we are likely to regard the stories of our inner life as poetic in character, the product of fancy; so we call them myths, contrasting them with the surer knowledge of fact which we believe ourselves to possess as rational observers of external events. Then Christianity is classified with poetry not only in the true sense, as dealing with selves, values and enduring time, but also in the wrong sense as permitting poetic license and the use of fictions in its explanation of history. This allocation of reason and imagination to separate spheres is doubly false, for in our knowledge of the external world we must employ imagination and in our interpretation of inner history we cannot get along without reason. Reason and imagination are both necessary in both spheres.

The rôle which imagination plays in the natural sciences is so great that some notable practitioners of the scientific method are inclined to believe that their pictures of the world are wholly poetic. In our ordinary lay knowledge of nature we find it necessary to use imagination constantly in order that we may interpret the bits of sensation which come to us. The jostling mob of confused, unintelligible, meaningless, visual and auditory sensations is made to march in order by a mind which approaches and apprehends them with some total image. We hasten to meet the sensations that come to us with anticipations of our own. We do not hear isolated ejaculations, separate and therefore meaningless words but apprehend each sound in a context that we in part supply. By means of ideas we interpret as we sense, and sense as we interpret. We anticipate connections between sensations before they are given and through imagination supply what is lacking in the immediate datum. So we may apprehend the meaning of a brown, rough texture of certain size and shape as the bark of a tree, or as a tree, or even as an experience of the adaptation of life to its environment. In such knowing of things everything depends upon the continuous conversation between sensation and imagination. We are not easily deceived by sensation but are fooled by a false imagination which interprets some sense-datum as part of a whole context to which it does not belong according to repeated, critical and common experience. By using concepts, images, patterns—be they visual images or the refined symbols of language and mathematics—which do not apply to the experience at hand we are led to false expectations and to inept reactions. In the darkness a perverse imagination interprets the visual impression of one side and section of the tree trunk so as to make a ghost out of the whole; in a moment of inattention I accept the word "bark" as part of a sentence about a dog rather than about a tree. In these cases it is not sensation but imagination which has been in error. Reason does not dispense with imagination but seeks to employ apt images and patterns whereby an otherwise inscrutable sensation becomes a true symbol of a reality whose other aspects, as anticipated in the image, are available to common experience. The main sources of error in such knowledge of nature seem to be the use of false images, the purely reflective combination of images and patterns in the mind without constant reference to sensation in which mental expectations are fulfilled or denied, and such an absolute identification of images with things that all criticism of the former is made impossible and all response to the latter is channeled in customary ways. In our external knowledge reason is right imagination; far from ruling out imagination reason depends upon its development, so that those most ethereal of poets, the pure mathematicians, become the spies of man's intelligence service and the pioneers of his dominion over nature.

In the internal knowledge of ourselves in our own history reason and imagination are similarly combined. Here the brute data which compare with sensations in external knowledge are the affections of the self. Pain and pleasure here are not physical states primarily; what is important about them is that they are *ours;* they occur in *our* bodies, directly or sympathetically, and so become joys and sorrows of the self; they are states of the soul. Nothing happens without the participation of our bodies, but the affections of the soul come to us through and in our social body almost as much as in our individual structure. We suffer with and in our community and there we also rejoice. With joys and sorrows, fears, hopes, loves, hates, pride, humility, and anger combine. And none of these affections remains uninterpreted. We meet each one with an imagination whereby we supply what is lacking in the immediate datum and are enabled to respond, rightly or wrongly, to a whole of reality of which this affection is for us a symbol and a part. In this realm all our images seem to be personal. We cannot think here with the aid of impersonal ideas; we cannot use machines as our models or mathematical formulae as our patterns. Inevitably, though we be disciplined in our external knowledge never to use the images of persons, when we interpret affections of the soul we use subjects for our ideas. This use of imagination is something quite different from mythology, which is the employment of personal images in objective knowledge where it is always deceptive, leading to unfulfillable expectations and to inept actions on external objects. The question which is relevant for the life of the self among selves is not whether personal images should be employed but only what personal images are right and adequate and which are evil imaginations of the heart.

Evil imaginations in this realm are shown to be evil by their consequences to selves and communities just as erroneous concepts and hypotheses in external knowledge are shown to be fallacious by their results. Some instances of evil imaginations of the heart will assist toward the clarification of the relationship between imagination and reason in this sphere. In various forms of insanity imagination and reason are not lacking but wrong images are employed by reason. The deluded person interprets all that happens to him but does so by means of inept patterns. His fears are real but he regards them as symbols of a great persecution directed against him; his hopes are signs of his greatness; his emotions of love may be indications to him of a mythical marriage. The images are false; his interpretations are unsupported by what other members of his community experience; hence he cuts himself off and is cut off from commerce with others and retires at last into the frustration of utter solitude. The case is similar with all those feelings of superiority and inferiority which blight the lives of men. An evil imagination of the heart interprets every sorrow as due to the pride of others or the inadequacy of the self; imagination deepens the sense of injury while responses are of a sort that increases the alienation of the person from his companions. In the social sphere the prevalence of such images is all too apparent to our time. The sorrows of the poor—no matter how much an external analysis accounts for their poverty by reference to economic movements and dislocations—are personal sorrows which require a personal explanation and this is offered in the image of wilfully selfish capitalists against whom emotions of personal anger are aroused. No less do the rich with their own woes—so poorly based to the external view on physical pain—imagine foreign agitators, trade unionists, statesmen and politicians to be responsible for their discontent and act accordingly. Again the image of the depraved race, now in the form of a Semitic, now of a Germanic, now of a Negro, now of a Japanese people, is used for the interpretation of social and individual sorrow. These are evil imaginations, resulting in continued conflict, in the impoverishment and destruction of selves both as agents and as sufferers. They present us with a world of confused personal agencies; these pluralistic patterns refuse to be combined into an integrated system. The images vary from day to day, from person to person. Arbitrariness and isolated subjectivity are the characteristic features of the world of selves understood by means of these imaginations of the heart. The animism of primitive life has its counterpart in every period of human history.

The image which the heart or the practical reason employs above all others in apprehending and understanding its affections is that of a dramatic action in which the self is the protagonist. Egotism is not only a characteristic of the will but also of the imagination, and appears in the tendency of the person to impute to all other selves the same interest in itself which it feels. In religion the joys and sorrows of the soul are referred to God as their source but God is thought to cause joy and sorrow purely because of his pleasure or displeasure in the self. Every pain raises the question, "How have I displeased him?" and every joy is thought to be based on a favor which is due to the self's meritorious action. The group also thinks of itself as in the center. So all nations tend to regard themselves as chosen peoples. Defeated or victorious they only become more aware of themselves, using both pain and pleasure to fortify themselves in the conviction that all the world is centered in their destiny. Such imagination can never enter into the knowledge of another self; it is always the "I" that is known and never the "Thou." The self lives in a real isolation in which others serve only as mirrors in which the ego is reflected. Moreover the picture of the self which this imagination uses is likely to be a wholly fanciful one, since it is not subject to the criticism of other selves.

These images of an animistic and self-centered world, whether in ancient or modern forms, are unable to make sense out of our history and our fate. Though they be applicable within narrow limits when they are subordinate to grander hypotheses, they leave great areas of life unexplained and when they are the ultimate images of the heart they lead to confusion and disaster. When we reason with their aid most sufferings and joys remain unintelligible. Evil and selfhood are left as mysteries. Solipsism in thought and action or irrational pluralism in theory and practice are the consequences. The impoverishment and alienation of the self, as well as the destruction of others, issues from a reasoning of the heart that uses evil imaginations.

This seems to be our situation in the world of selves apart from revelation. We have some patterns which we can employ in understanding our joys and sorrows but for the most part they are not only inadequate, leaving us ignorant, but evil, tending to lead to destruction.

When we see the errors in animistic and self-centered reasoning we are tempted to turn away entirely from conceptions which make use of the idea of selves. We try to employ in the understanding of personal relations the images which we have learned to use with some success in our external,

non-participating knowledge of things. We seek
to understand ourselves and others as beings without selves—things that are to be understood in a
context of things. So we interpret the criminal as
the necessary end-product of a series of hereditary
and environmental causes. We speak of those who
cause us pain as maladjusted persons and use the
same figure of speech in explaining our own sins
and sorrows. The word is significant, for adjust-
ments and maladjustments are primarily operations
carried out on things without their consent or participation. We interpret the conflict between rich
and poor as the consequence of economic evolution
in which impersonal factors are decisive; machines
and markets, conditions of production and distribu-
tion rather than the good or evil wills of men account for the miseries of the proletariat and the
fears of the bourgeoisie. Nations are understood as
geographic, biological and economic units that cannot help being what they are and doing what they
do. They are to be dealt with, therefore, without
praise and blame as one deals with undernourished
bodies or with maladjusted carburetors. We use
similar images to understand the history of our religion or of our church. So the heart reasons with
ideas borrowed from the head; the participant in
life uses the images of an observer of life's external
aspects. When we think in this way it is unnecessary to refer to revelation as the intuition of a spe-

cial occasion; the concepts we employ are related to no particular occasion but are impersonal, quantitative and non-historical.

The intimate relations which obtain between the pure and the practical reasons, between the contemplative and the participating lives, doubtless make such impersonal reasoning necessary and fruitful. Physiological, economic and psychological interpretations of men, races and nations are an inescapable element in all responsible dealing with persons and communities. But that the mechanical or at least impersonal model of the observer is a myth when used primarily or exclusively in understanding and responding to selves two considerations indicate quite clearly. The first is that no man in the situation of a participant in life actually succeeds in interpreting and dealing with other human beings on this level; the second is that the impersonal account leaves large areas of our experience unrationalized and uncontrolled.

Many illustrations of the first point may be found in history. The inconsistency which is an element in every great philosophy that begins with observation and ends with action bears testimony to the inadequacy of the impersonal point of view. When Plato turns seriously from philosophy to politics, as in the *Laws*, the forms or ideas yield their preeminent place to God and the soul. When Spinoza makes his transition from metaphysics to ethics and seeks to show men a way of salvation he does not succeed in keeping his images of man and God on the impersonal plane. The so-called scientific socialism of Marx abandons the impersonal images of the social process as soon as it moves to action. As active revolutionaries, communists do not regard the might of the proletariat as the historically relative product of economic evolution and the basis of their right; rather they believe that this might has a right to be mighty because it will establish universal equality, freedom and happiness. Moving to action they abandon the position of spectators for whom capitalists must simply be what they are and now blame them for being unjust. Valency is transformed into value for persons, and instead of impersonal processes personal motives are analyzed when the transition is made from external knowledge to participation. Scientific humanism, also, must actually give up the interpretation of human relations in impersonal terms when it proceeds to action, no matter how much it denies in words the fact that it does so. A psychologist choosing his vocation or promising to love and cherish a life-partner cannot act on the hypothesis that there is no consciousness of self and no self but only an impersonal process of mind or matter. In decision and action the images used in observation are inept and must actually give way to ideas of selves and of values for selves. Positivists who affirm that terms of praise and blame are meaningless yet tend in times of dispute with those whom they call obscurantists to praise and blame as if there were persons before them and as if there were a value in their own view, as if truth made a difference to persons. A strange blindness often afflicts those who believe that they employ the strictly impersonal and descriptive method in all affairs of life; they do not see how they abandon this method themselves in every decision to publish their ideas and in all their identification of themselves with their thoughts. The participant in life simply cannot escape thinking in terms of persons and of values. It would be possible to do so only if he could depersonalize the self, become a body without an inner life, without joys and sorrows, loves and hates, without neighbors, without hope or fear —a thing in a world of things. But in such a world no truth would ever need to be uttered; existence without worth or unworthiness would be all in all. The images of the observational method are so out of place in the life of participation that they must be abandoned in favor of other ideas or surreptitiously modified when employed by moral agents in moments of decisive action.

The alternative to inconsistency in this transition from the method of observation to personal participation, while employing the impersonal patterns of thought relevant to the former, is the abandonment of the practical, moral life to the irrationality of passion or of custom. Some positivists dismiss all judgments about value, all religious affirmations, all references to selves as meaningless because they cannot be translated into words referring to sense-experience or because they cannot be understood by means of the impersonal images of natural science. Morality, politics, religion are simply unintelligible and irrational, they say. But the actuality of value-judgments, of religious devotion, of self-consciousness and consciousness of other selves, of the world of relations between selves, cannot be dismissed with the statement that these things are unintelligible. The consequence of declaring any part of human experience and action to be beyond reason is not to eliminate it from existence but to leave it subject to unregulated passion, to uncriticized custom, or to the evil imaginations of the heart. Anyone who affirms the irrationality of the moral and religious life simply abandons the effort to discipline this life, to find right images by means of which to understand himself, his sorrows and joys. Such positivism leaves the door of human moral life wide open to the appearance of anarchy and the sway of primitive emotion accompanied by primitive mythology. The way out of the dilemma which many exponents of this way of thinking adopt is to accept and to advise their disciples to follow the customary morality of the group in which they live. Thereby they acknowledge the reality of the moral, practical life and the limitation of their rational method to the world of things; but they allow custom to pursue its uncriticized way, surrendering the effort to discover and to extend the power of rational principles in it.

These considerations, among others, indicate not that the life of personal selves is beyond reason but that the patterns which pure or scientific reason employs in understanding the behavior of things are inapplicable to the personal sphere. If ethics, politics, religion—the whole complex of personal relations—are to be understood and rescued from the rule of chance imagination, if they are to be made "scientific," it must be by some other method than through the transfer to them of images and patterns employed by contemplative reason observing a world of things. The errors and superstitions fostered by bad imagination in this realm cannot be overcome by eliminating ideas of self and of value for selves but only by more adequate images of the same order.

The heart must reason; the participating self cannot escape the necessity of looking for pattern and meaning in its life and relations. It cannot make a choice between reason and imagination but only between reasoning on the basis of adequate images and thinking with the aid of evil imaginations.

Neither the primitive images of animism nor the impersonal patterns of modern scientific, or indeed of any kind of purely contemplative, thought supply a basis for the rational understanding of the self in its community and history. But there is an image neither evil nor inadequate which enables the heart to understand and the event through which that image is given them Christians call their revelation.

II. *Interpretation through Revelation*

By revelation in our history, then, we mean that special occasion which provides us with an image by means of which all the occasions of personal and common life become intelligible. What concerns us at this point is not the fact that the revelatory moment shines by its own light and is intelligible in itself but rather that it illuminates other events and enables us to understand them. Whatever else revelation means it does mean an event in our history which brings rationality and wholeness into the confused joys and sorrows of personal existence and allows us to discern order in the brawl of communal histories. Such revelation is no substitute for reason; the illumination it supplies does not excuse the mind from labor; but it does give to that mind the impulsion and the first principles it requires if it is to be able to do its proper work. In this sense we may say that the revelatory moment is revelatory because it is rational, because it makes the understanding of order and meaning in personal history possible. Through it a pattern of dramatic unity becomes apparent with the aid of which the heart can understand what has happened, is happening and will happen to selves in their community. Why we must call this a dramatic pattern and how it differs from the conceptual patterns of the observer's reason can be most clearly indicated through an examination of the way in which the heart uses it to understand life's meaning.

First of all, the revelatory moment is one which makes our past intelligible. Through it we understand what we remember, remember what we have forgotten and appropriate as our own past much that seemed alien to us. In the life of an individual a great occasion may make significant and intelligible the apparently haphazard course of his earlier existence; all that has happened to him may then assume continuity and pattern as it is related to the moment for which he knows himself to have been born. So prophets, being called to prophecy, may understand with Jeremiah how birth and nurture were for them an ordination to their office or an Augustine may see blessing even in the "sin which brought so great a salvation." When Israel focussed its varied and disordered recollections of a nomad past, of tribal bickerings and alien tyrannies in the revelatory event of its deliverance and choice to be a holy people, then it found there hitherto unguessed meaning and unity. What had been a "tale told by an idiot, full of sound and fury, signifying nothing," became a grand epic; every line, stanza and canto fell into its proper place. The tribal chants, the legends of the unheroic past were not forgotten; they were remembered in a new connection; meanings hitherto hidden became clear. To be sure, the labor of prophets and poets and priests who searched the memories of Israel and ordered them with the aid of the revelatory image was necessary before a unified understanding could be achieved. They had to carry the light of revelation into their past; revelation did not excuse the reasoning heart from toil but equipped it with the instrument whereby it could understand what it remembered. So the Scriptures were written not as the history of revelation only but as the history of Israel understood and unified by means of revelation. The labor of Israel in seeking to understand the past has never been completed, being continued by the rabbis of a later and the present day; but the revelatory occasion and idea have remained constant.

In the Christian church the function of the revelation in Jesus Christ has been similar. Through it the early apostles understood and interpreted the memories not only of Hebrew but also of Gentile Christians. The whole past of the human race assumed for them a unity and significance that had been lacking in the national and religious recollections of men. That Jesus had been born in the fullness of time meant that all things which had gone before seemed to conspire toward the realization of this event. Not only the religion of the Hebrews but the philosophy of the Greeks also was now intelligible as prophecy of the coming of a great salvation. The work of the apostles has been carried on through the following ages of the church. The rise and fall of pagan empires as well as the destiny of the chosen people, Socrates' martyrdom as well as Jeremiah's, the wanderings of Greeks as well as of Hebrews, have come to be understood not simply as illustrations of a general principle of creative love and judgment in history but as parts of one inclusive process. The work has not been completed, for the past is infinite, and thought, even with the aid of revelation, is painful, and doubt assails the human heart. But for the Christian church the whole past is potentially a single epic. In the presence of the revelatory occasion it can and must remember in tranquillity the long story of human ascent from the dust, of descent into the sloughs of brutality and sin, the nameless sufferings of untold numbers of generations, the groaning and travailing of creation until now—all that otherwise is remembered only with despair. There is no part of that past that can be ignored or regarded as beyond possibility of redemption from meaninglessness. And it is the ability of the revelation to save all the past from senselessness that is one of the marks of its revelatory character.

By reasoning on the basis of revelation the heart not only understands what it remembers but is enabled and driven to remember what it had forgotten. When we use insufficient and evil images of the personal or social self we drop out of our consciousness or suppress those memories which do not fit in with the picture of the self we cherish. We bury our follies and our transgressions of our own law, our departures from our own ideal, in the depths of our unconsciousness. We also forget much that seems to us trivial, since it does not make sense when interpreted by means of the idolatrous image. We do not destroy this past of ours; it is indestructible. We carry it with us; its record is written deep into our lives. We only refuse to acknowledge it as our true past and try to make it an alien thing—something that did not happen to our real selves. So our national histories do not recall to the consciousness of citizens the crimes and absurdities of past social conduct, as our written and unwritten autobiographies fail to mention our shame. But this unremembered past endures. An external view can see its embodiment in the boundaries of nations, in the economic status of groups, such as that of Negroes in America, in folkways and customs whose origins have been forgotten, in national policies and in personal habits. When we live and act in accordance with our inward social constitution in which there are class and race divisions, prejudices, assumptions about the things we can and cannot do, we are constrained by the unconscious past. Our buried past is mighty; the ghosts of our fathers and of the selves that we have been haunt our days and nights though we refuse to acknowledge their presence.

The revelatory event resurrects this buried past. It demands and permits that we bring into the light of attention our betrayals and denials, our follies and sins. There is nothing in our lives, in our autobiographies and our social histories, that does not fit in. In the personal inner life revelation requires the heart to recall the sins of the self and to confess fully what it shuddered to remember. Every great confession, such as Augustine's or St. Paul's, indicates how this rationalizing of the past takes place. And every social history, not least that of the church itself, when recollected in the light of revelation, becomes a confession of sin. It is true that in this realm the work of revelation has never been completed and that, indeed, in many spheres it has not even been started. Yet it is also true that for Christians critical history of self and community, wherein the forgotten past is recollected, is the possible and necessary consequence of revelation.

The third function of revelation with respect to

the past we may call appropriation. When men enter into a new community they not only share the present life of their new companions but also adopt as their own the past history of their fellows. So immigrants do not become true members of the American community until they have learned to call the Pilgrims and the men of 1776 their fathers and to regard the torment of the Civil War as somehow their own. Where common memory is lacking, where men do not share in the same past there can be no real community, and where community is to be formed common memory must be created; hence the insistence on the teaching of history in modern national communities. But by the aid of such provincial memories only partial pasts can be appropriated and only limited human communities can be formed. To Christians the revelatory moment is not only something they can all remember as having happened in their common past, be they Hebrews or Greeks, slaves or free, Europeans or Africans or Americans or Asiatics, medieval men or modern. It becomes an occasion for appropriating as their own the past of all human groups. Through Jesus Christ Christians of all races recognize the Hebrews as their fathers; they build into their lives as Englishmen or as Americans, as Italians or Germans, the memories of Abraham's loyalty, of Moses' heroic leadership, of prophetic denunciations and comfortings. All that has happened to the strange and wandering people of God becomes a part of their own past. But Jesus Christ is not only the Jew who suffered for the sins of Jews and so for our own sins; he is also the member of the Roman world-community through whom the Roman past is made our own. The history of empire through which his life and death must be understood is the history of our empire. Beyond all that, he is the man through whom the whole of human history becomes our history. Now there is nothing that is alien to us. All the struggles, searchings after light, all the wanderings of all the peoples, all the sins of men in all places become parts of our past through him. We must remember them all as having happened in and to our community. Through Christ we become immigrants into the empire of God which extends over all the world and learn to remember the history of that empire, that is of men in all times and places, as our history.

Such interpretation and apprehension of our past, such rationalization of all that has happened in our history is not an intellectual exercise but a moral event. The heart of the participating self is engaged in this work and through it the soul is reconstructed. For the past which we remember through Jesus Christ is not the serial but the enduring past. When we speak of the past in internal history we do not refer to events which no longer have reality in the world; we mean our constitution, our enduring inheritance. Our past is what we are, since what we are now is the impulse and the go, the habit, custom, commitment to community and principle, which an external view refers to causes no longer existent but which from the internal viewpoint have their origin and meaning in the self and its community. Our past is our present in the drives, desires, instincts which an external view traces to our animal origin; it is present in the ways of social behavior that an observing history derives from forces operative long ago but which make us what we are. Our past is our present in our conscious and unconscious memory. To understand such a present past is to understand one's self and, through understanding, to reconstruct. The apprehension and interpretation of our living past through the revelatory moment may be likened to the psychiatrist's method of seeking to induce a total recall on the part of a patient or of bringing into the light of day what had been a source of anguish while it remained suppressed. To remember all that is in our past and so in our present is to achieve unity of self. To remember the human past as our own past is to achieve community with mankind. Such conversion of the memory is an important, indispensable part of the soul's conversion. Without the integration of the personal and social past there can be no present integrity of the self nor anything like human brotherhood. Through Jesus

Christ Christians can and must turn again and again to history, making the sins and the faiths of their fathers and brothers their own faiths and sins.

That such conversion is not easily completed but rather a permanent revolutionary movement is evident. It must go on throughout the whole of a life-time because the past is infinite and because sin enters anew in repeated efforts to separate ourselves from God and our fellow-men through the separation of our past from them. So the Christian church sins anew in separating its past from that of the Hebrews, or in attempting to eliminate from its history part of the common life, as when Protestants try to forget medieval Christian history or Catholics regard the development since the Reformation as no true part of their story. The conversion of the past must be continuous because the problems of reconciliation arise in every present. Today, for instance, the reconciliation of the various parties and sections of the Christian church is not only desirable but imperative. The obstacles to that reunion are multifarious, but one of the greatest of them is that every part of disunited Christendom interprets its past through an image of itself and holds fast without repentance to that image. It carries with it a great wealth and burden of tradition, but acknowledges and confesses only that part of it which fits in with a self-centered image. Hence each part of Christendom is unable to understand what other parts mean with their theologies, rituals, orders and systems of ethics. Moreover the groups use their separate histories as means for defending themselves against the criticism of others and as weapons for warfare upon rival parties. We cannot become integrated parts of one common church until we each remember our whole past, with its sins, through Jesus Christ and appropriate each other's pasts. There will be no union of Catholics and Protestants until through the common memory of Jesus Christ the former repent of the sin of Peter and the latter of the sin of Luther, until Protestants acknowledge Thomas Aquinas as one of their fathers, the Inquisition as their own sin and Ignatius Loyola as one of their own Reformers, until Catholics have canonized Luther and Calvin, done repentance for Protestant nationalism, and appropriated Schleiermacher and Barth as their theologians. In the narrower sphere of Protestant reunion this work of reconstructing the past through Jesus Christ must go on very diligently before we can be truly one. No mere desire to overcome differences of opinion is of any avail unless it expresses itself in such reinterpretation and appropriation of what lies back of opinion—the memory. The adoption of John Wesley into their own history by Anglicans, of Calvin and Zwingli by Lutherans, of Fox and Woolman by orthodox Protestants is not only a necessary prelude to union; it is union. All such

recall and interpretation of the past is impossible
when we use the images of Luther, Wesley, Calvin
and Fox or of the segments of history connected
with such names. We cannot understand Calvin
through Fox nor Wesley through Laud. We need
a larger pattern, a more inclusive hypothesis
through which to understand each other's and our
own memories. Such a pattern we have in the revelation of Jesus Christ. In him we see the sin of man,
not of some men; in him we find the faith of man,
not of Protestants or Catholics, of Lutherans or
Presbyterians. He reveals the faith and the sin of
all the fathers of all the churches; through him we
can repent of our own fathers' sins and gratefully
adopt as our own the faithful, sinful fathers of those
from whom we are now separated.

The problem of human reunion is greater than
the problem of church reunion. It also must be approached through memory. The measure of our
distance from each other in our nations and groups
can be taken by noting the divergence, the separate-
ness and lack of sympathy in our social memories.
Conversely the measure of our unity is the extent of
our common memory. As in the United States,
North and South give evidence of present disorder
through the recollection of sectional histories and
bear witness to union through histories wherein
Lee is a national hero and Lincoln a common de-
liverer, so in mankind national histories testify to

actual animosities or isolations while common memories indicate true peace. Our human history cannot be reconstructed save with the aid of repentance and faith; none of the national images men employ in interpreting and recalling their past suffice to bring unity. But in Jesus Christ Christians recall and appropriate as their own all that men have done and suffered in the one human world where there are neither Jews nor Greeks, neither Orientals nor Occidentals.

Revelation does not accomplish the work of conversion; the reasoning heart must search out memory and bring to light forgotten deeds. But without the revelatory image this work does not seem possible. In the reconstruction of our living past revelation is the hand-maid of reason; yet the figure is misleading for the partnership is not one of mastery and servitude but of indispensable co-operation. Without revelation reason is limited and guided into error; without reason revelation illuminates only itself.

The heart must reason not only about and in the past but in the present too. We do not call those events in our history revelation which cast no light upon the things that are happening to us or which we now do in the company of other selves. If our past in inner history is everything we carry with us, or what we are, our present is our action, our doing and our suffering of deeds done to us. As an evil imagination hides from us what we are so it also obscures what we are doing. The words of Jesus on the cross, "Father, forgive them, they know not what they do," are applicable to us in every moment. We are particularly aware of this in times of great social crisis when our complacent dogmatism is shattered and we realize that what is going on and what we are participating in is too great for our imagination or interpretation. We have no pattern of personal thought inclusive and clear enough to allow us to discern any orderly connections between the wild and disturbed actions of men and nations. We do not know what we are doing by our aggressions and participations, our inactions and isolations from conflict. We move from day to day, from moment to moment, and are often blown about by many winds of political and social doctrine. What the sources and what the issues of our deeds and sufferings may be remains obscure.

In our smaller communities, in our families and with our friends the same ignorance is our portion. We do not know as parents, save in fragmentary ways, what we are doing to our children. We do not understand what our most intimate friends, or our husbands and wives are doing to us and neither do they know.

As we move about among these mists we employ imaginations of the heart to make intelligible in a narrow sphere the actions and sufferings of selves.

So we interpret international events by means of the pattern of a national peace, conceiving this peace as absence of disturbance of our customary conduct, or we use the ancient image of the war between darkness and light to understand and justify our defense and aggression. We understand the meaning of strikes and of unemployment with the aid of an hypothesis which makes our continued possession of advantages or otherwise, the victory of our class, the central value. We use the images of French or Russian Revolutions, with accent on the fate of persons, as the concepts by means of which to understand what is going on. Ideal patterns of domestic peace, of parental authority, of mother love or friendly loyalty become the explanations of what we are doing and suffering. In all this effort to understand or at least to justify our actions the self is likely to remain the central figure. We explain ourselves by ourselves or by means of the picture we have made of ourselves. So in the Christian church we dramatize our selves, thinking of this community as the world's savior by great deeds of teaching or noble sufferings. But with the aid of such patterns we succeed more in obscuring than in illuminating what we are doing.

This becomes apparent when we bring to bear upon our actions the larger image given us in revelation. Through the cross of Christ we gain a new

understanding of the present scene; we note relations previously ignored; find explanations of our
actions hitherto undreamed of. Deeds and sufferings begin to compose themselves into a total picture of significant action in which the self no longer
occupies the center. We now begin to comprehend
the tragedy of contemporary life as a connected,
unified affair in which one act succeeds another
by a moral necessity in view of the great divine,
dominating purpose.

First of all, in interpreting our present, we use
the life and death of Christ as a parable and an analogy. The scribes and Pharisees now sit in Peter's
seat, and in the churches of St. Paul priests plot defense against the disturber of the people; disciples
are corrupted by thirty pieces of silver; moneychangers and those who sell human victims for
vain sacrifices conspire with Pilates who wash their
bloody hands in public; poor unreasoning soldiers
commit sins which are not their own; betrayals and
denials take place in every capital; and so, out of
cumulative self-deceit and treachery, out of great
ignorance, out of false fears and all the evil imaginations of the heart, crosses are constructed not
only for thieves but for the sons of God. We see
through the use of the great parable how bodies
are now being broken for our sake and how for the
remission of our sins the blood of innocents is being
shed. Not with complete clarity, to be sure, yet as

in a glass darkly, we can discern in the contemporary confusion of our lives the evidence of a pattern in which, by great travail of men and God, a work of redemption goes on which is like the work of Christ. We learn to know what we are doing and what is being done to us—how by an infinite suffering of the eternal victim we are condemned and forgiven at the same time; how an infinite loyalty refuses to abandon us either to evil or to nothingness, but works at our salvation with a tenacity we are tempted to deplore. The story of Jesus, and particularly of his passion, is the great illustration that enables us to say, "What we are now doing and suffering is like this."

Yet we employ the revelatory moment as more than parable or analogy. It is the rational image; by its means we not only try to understand what our actions and sufferings are like, but what they really are. In theology, therefore, we tend to turn away from the preacher's use of the great history as parable and to think in conceptual terms. From the great occasion we abstract general ideas of an impersonal character which we find illustrated also in other occasions. So we speak of original sin and the forgiveness of sins, of reconciliation, of the principle of obedience as manifested in Jesus, of the meaning of suffering in general. The revelatory moment now is not itself the rational image but affords opportunity for the discovery of concepts

of great generality whereby we are enabled to explain contemporary action in the moral or personal realm. Revelation now is concentrated in
doctrines and it seems possible to state these without reference to the historic occasion in which
they first became evident. As in natural science
it is not necessary to remember the person of New-
ton and the incidents of his life in order that the
theory of gravitation may be employed, so it would
appear that in theology we do not need to use the
historic event in order to apply ideas which became
evident through it but are independent of it.
Theology, thinking in this fashion, is then inclined
to identify revelation with the publication in an
historic moment of great doctrines or ideas.

The course of Christian thought through the
centuries indicates, however, that there is something very unsatisfactory about such abstraction
of general ideas from the great occasion and that
the preacher's use of the dramatic image comes
nearer the requirements of the reasoning heart than
does the theologian's application of a conceptual
pattern. Despite repeated efforts to state theological ideas abstractly it has been necessary for the
church to return again and again to statements
about historic actuality. It will not do, apparently,
to define revelation in a dual fashion as the "intuition of special occasions" and the reception of concepts by means of which all occasions can be eluci-

dated. The relation between the special occasion and all other occasions is more intimate or the concepts possess a generality differing from that which belongs to the impersonal ideas of contemplative reason. Theology cannot speak simply of general ideas of sonship to God, of forgiveness of sins, of obedience to death, of humility or *kenosis*, as illustrated in the great occasion and elsewhere. It must speak of a unique sonship, a unique obedience, a single sacrifice. The revelatory occasion, it appears, does not simply illustrate great uniformities of divine and human behavior—though it does that also—but exhibits a unique, unrepetitive pattern. Hence there arises a seeming dilemma for theology and the church. Revelation, it appears, must either mean the general ideas through which we understand our present human world in its relations, its actions and sufferings, but then it cannot mean the historic occasion in our memory save as an illustration; or revelation means the historic occasion and then it cannot explain present experience save in analogical or parabolic fashion.

The dilemma, however, appears to be somewhat unreal when we recall that the reality we are dealing with and trying to understand is our history, in which we seek less for uniformities of behavior than for a principle of unity in a duration. Concepts which describe the recurrent features in events are necessary for that external contemplation of our

lives to which we must return frequently in order
that we may put checks on the inner imagination.
But the real work of reason in our history is that
of understanding in terms of persons, communities
and values what we are doing and suffering. In this
history, time is duration and unrepetitive in character. Here we try to understand, not how features
in our past are repeated in our present, but how
our present grows out of our past into our future.
A traveller on the road does not undertake to discover what he is doing, where his road is taking
him, by remembering similar occasions in his past
and by abstracting from them general ideas. Conceptual knowledge, indeed, can be of help to him
as when he uses the compass and consults the sun's
position. But no such general knowledge will let
him understand the position of the city he seeks,
the relation of the place he occupies to human
habitations, to his own purposes, fears and hopes.
To understand his present situation he needs a map
of the individual, unimitated territory in which he
is travelling; he needs to recall whence he came and
what the direction of his particular journey. He
must reason with the aid of an image that is unique
though mental. The revelation which we use to
understand our present situation and what we are
now doing is more like such a map than like a dic-
tionary through which we seek to understand the
meaning of words frequently repeated.

We may employ other parables to clarify to our-selves how we actually employ the revelatory mo-ment as a rational principle for the understanding of present experience. Revelation is like a classic drama which, through the events of one day and place, makes intelligible the course of a family his-tory. Or it is like a decisive moment in the common life of friends. In the face of some emergency a man may act so as to reveal a quality undisclosed before. Through that revelatory moment his friend is enabled to understand past actions which had been obscure and to prophesy the future behavior of the revealer. But the revealing moment not only disclosed constant features of conduct which had previously been hidden; it also introduced a new relation between the persons and remains a unique point in their history. Again, a conversation be-tween friends can become very confused so that they do not understand each other. In such a situa-tion they not only seek to define their words but go back to a critical point in their dialogue, starting once more to think from that beginning. So when we attempt to interpret our present experience by means of revelation we return to a critical point in man's conversation with God and try to under-stand the present as a continuation from that be-ginning. The law-books and dictionaries which describe the content of divine prescriptions or the meaning of divine words are helpful yet of secondary importance in our attempt to understand what we are doing and where we are. Concepts and doctrines derived from the unique historical moment are important but less illuminating than the occasion itself. For what is revealed is not so much the mode of divine behavior as the divine self.

We reason in our hearts in order that we may know the whither as well as the whence and where of our personal lives. If the past in inner history is what we are and the present what we do, our future is our potentiality. Through revelation we seek to discover what is implicit in our lives and will become explicit. And the revelation which illuminates our sin prophesies our death, the death of self and that of the community. The small, deceitful patterns of false prophecy will always assure us that we and our communities are immortal, that the worth of our selves is so great that they cannot die and the value of our chosen peoples so immense that they will last forever. But in the light of revelation we see the end because we discern the beginning of the end in the present. No honest Old Testament prophet ever promised eternal joy to his nation save on the other side of disaster. Much less can an honest New Testament prophet, using the cross of Christ for his understanding of human fate, predict for men and societies immortality without judgment. To show up as clearly as may be the potentiality of catastrophe in our lives is as much a function of reason using revelation in our day as in any ancient time.

Yet in the light of the revelatory occasion the Christian discerns another possibility; it is not his own possibility in the sense that it is implicit in him. But it is possible to the person who reveals himself in the historic occasion as the Lord of life and death. It is the possibility of the resurrection of a new and other self, of a new community, a reborn remnant.

Thus the heart reasons with the aid of revelation. All reasoning is painful and none more so than that which leads to knowledge of the self. In the Christian community we do not use our revelation faithfully but seek by a thousand devices to escape from this rational understanding of ourselves. By means of dogmatism which assures us that nothing more is necessary to our knowledge than the creeds supply, or by means of a scepticism which declares all things unintelligible, we seek to evade the necessity of illuminating and reconstructing our memories and acts. Sometimes we regard revelation as though it had equipped us with truth in such measure that no further labor in historical and psychological searching is necessary; sometimes we dismiss it as offering no basis for the reason of man. Fundamentalism in its thousand historic forms escapes in one way; modernism, which exists in as many disguises as there are climates of opinion, escapes

by applying to life the short and narrow ideas of
some present moment. Emotionalism reduces the
historic revelation to a demagogic device for arous-
ing fear, anger and pity in the service of some petty
cause. The figures of the Christian drama are even
made to act out the puerile and vicious farces of
racial, nationalistic and ecclesiastic imaginations.
But revelation is not the source of such irrationality
and absurdity. We become fools because we refuse
to use revelation as the foundation of a rational
moral life.

III. *Progressive Revelation*

A revelation which furnishes the practical reason with a starting point for the interpretation of
past, present and future history is subject to progressive validation. The more apparent it becomes
that the past can be understood, recovered and integrated by means of a reasoning starting with
revelation, the more contemporary experience is
enlightened and response to new situations aptly
guided by this imagination of the heart, the more a
prophecy based on this truth is fulfilled, the surer
our conviction of its reality becomes. In this respect
as in many others, Christian revelation is like the
revelation of Hebrew faith. The prophets saw God
acting in and through the actions of the nations of
their own time by apprehending these as repetition
and even more as a continuation of the mighty acts

whereby the Lord had delivered Israel from bondage. Priests reconstructed history until they saw the past, not only of Judah but of all Israel, not only of Israel but of all mankind, as one past and one preparation for the saving work of God. And seers prophesied with strange accuracy events to come, not by observing the movement of planets and stars or by adding mystic numbers, but by making explicit what was implicit in the relations of a sinful nation with a just and holy God. Revelation was not only validated but every new event and every reinterpreted memory became a part of revelation since in all events the same Lord appeared and was known of men. So history based on revelation became a history of revelation.

It is not otherwise with the revelation to which the church refers. It is progressively validated in the individual Christian life as ever new occasions are brought under its light, as sufferings and sins, as mercies and joys are understood by its aid. Revelation has been tested in this way by many generations of men and its success in clarifying and reconstructing souls is one source of its great prestige among us. Moreover such validation has been more than proof of the initial principle, for every event which the revelatory moment clarified has been in a sense a repetition and continuation of that moment so that Christians have been able to say long after the first generation, "That which was from the beginning, which we have heard, which we have seen with our eyes, which we have looked upon, and our hands have handled, of the Word of life; . . . that which we have seen and heard declare we unto you, that ye also may have fellowship with us."

It cannot be denied that there have been many failures in the application of the method of revelation, that through long periods the reasoning heart of Christianity has remained content with ancient understanding, or that the very idea of the revelation of a living God has been lost in the effort to confine revelation to a set of customary ecclesiastical assertions about God and man. There has been a marked hesitancy in the modern period to apply the method of revelation to the history of societies or communities as though the gospel applied only to men in isolated communion with God. The common life has, therefore, been interpreted by means of other images less inclusive and often evil. In particular the social gospel has often brought to bear on societies only the impoverished image of a conflict between good and evil in which victory is not by grace but by merit, in which there is no suffering of the son of God nor forgiveness for the sinful society. But the failures of the church to use its method are not the fault of the method. Indeed, when the church recognizes the revelatory moment as truly revelatory it is impelled to continuing, progressive interpretation of every occasion in the life of men by means of its great image of the saving work of God. In our time particularly, with the manifest destruction being wrought by men with evil imaginations of the heart, Christians are sent back to the method of reasoning on the basis of revelation and can practice it with the firm expectancy that it will be able not only to illuminate contemporary life but also to give new assurance of the present activity of that same judging and loving God who manifested himself in Jesus Christ.

Revelation is not progressive in the sense that we can substitute for the revelatory moment of Jesus Christ some other moment in our history and interpret the latter through the former. The monastic movement and the Reformation, modern evangelism and the social gospel, represent no progress beyond the New Testament in the sense that we may understand the latter through the former. Benedict and Luther must be interpreted through Christ and not vice versa; modern civilization and modern human life must be regarded as the scene of activity on the part of the Father of Jesus Christ, but Jesus cannot be rightly understood as the son of the god of modern culture. Nevertheless revelation is a moving thing in so far as its meaning is realized only by being brought to bear upon the interpretation and reconstruction of ever new human situations in an enduring movement, a single drama of divine and human action. So the God who revealed himself continues to reveal himself—the one God of all times and places.

In another slightly different sense we may speak of revelation as progressive. First principles are not only our beginnings from which we proceed to second and third things; they are also our endings toward which we move from the multiplicity of present experience. In our conceptual knowledge we move back and forth from reason to experience and from experience back to reason. And in that dialectic of the mind our concepts are enriched, clarified and corrected no less than our experience is illuminated and directed. We do not easily change first principles but we discover more fully what they mean. By moving back from experience to the categories in our mind we find out more clearly what was in our mind. The reason of the heart engages in a similar dialectic, and it does not really know what is in the revelation, in the illuminating moment, save as it proceeds from it to present experience and back again from experience to revelation. In that process the meaning of the revelation, its richness and power, grow progressively clearer. This progressive understanding of revelation is also an infinite process. "To be assaulted by the presence of greatness," Professor Hocking writes in his *Thoughts on Life and Death*, "is not to take it in; a mountain makes no immediate impression of vastness—it conspires with the illusion of distance to conceal its proportions, and we only know them through the journey and the climb." We climb the mountain of revelation that we may gain a view of the shadowed valley in which we dwell and from the valley we look up again to the mountain. Each arduous journey brings new understanding, but also new wonder and surprise. This mountain is not one we climbed once upon a time; it is a well-known peak we never wholly know, which must be climbed again in every generation, on every new day. There is no time or place in human history, there is no moment in the church's past, nor is there any set of doctrines, any philosophy or theology of which we might say, "Here the knowledge possible through revelation and the knowledge of revelation is fully set forth." Revelation is not only progressive but it requires of those to whom it has come that they begin the never-ending pilgrim's progress of the reasoning Christian heart.

CHAPTER IV

THE DEITY OF GOD

I. *God Reveals Himself*

OUR attempt to achieve clarity about what we mean by revelation in the Christian community has proceeded by progressive stages from the definition of the standpoint to the description of the historic context and thence to that illuminated section of the latter whence light streams on obscurer portions. When we speak of revelation we mean that something has happened to us in our history which conditions all our thinking and that through this happening we are enabled to apprehend what we are, what we are suffering and doing and what our potentialities are. What is otherwise arbitrary and dumb fact becomes related, intelligible and eloquent fact through the revelatory event. To the extent that revelation furnishes the practical reason with an adequate starting point it may be said to be validated.

But the rational value of revelation is not its first value and its validation in the reasoning of the heart is not the primary validation. When we speak of revelation we do not mean that a tentative hypothesis, however great, has been offered to us and that this hypothesis must be validated by its fruitful use before it is acceptable. We do not mean that we have freely chosen one section of our history because we found that it made sense of the remainder. We mean rather that something has happened which compels our faith and which requires us to seek rationality and unity in the whole of our history. Revelation is like the kingdom of God; if we seek it first all other things are added to us but if we seek it for the sake of these other things we really deny it. The kingdom proves itself to be the kingdom of God not only by its immediate worth but also by its instrumental value in leading to secondary goods, and revelation proves itself to be revelation of reality not only by its intrinsic verity but also by its ability to guide men to many other truths. But the first value of revelation as of the kingdom is intrinsic and we begin with it not because it will lead to further knowledge but because it is itself the truth. When Descartes was led to doubt almost all the things he had believed, he returned in his mind to the one fixed point of his own existence as a thinker. He discovered, to be sure, that when he began with this certainty, reasoning from that starting point, many things became clear that had been previously obscure; yet the certainty of his existence was not dependent on the consequences to which it led; the assertion, "I think, therefore I am," possessed validity prior to its validation through the service it rendered as a starting point of thought about other things. So it is with revelation, and if it were not so we would remain forever dubious of the knowledge we derive from our use of it in our reasoning about our history. In our reasoning about selves and their destiny we use some hypotheses which may be dropped or corrected if experience does not agree with them. Theological systems and theories of revelation are of this order. But back of all such hypotheses there are convictions which are not subject to criticism, since they are the bases of all possible criticism. The situation is similar in natural science, which cannot abandon its faith in the intelligibility and unity of nature without destroying itself; neither can the certainty that mathematical relations are discernible in all phenomena be surrendered, though hypotheses setting forth this or that type of relationship may be given up. In dealing with revelation we refer to something in our history to which we always return as containing our first certainty. It is our "*cogito, ergo sum*," though it must be stated in the opposite way as, "I am being thought, therefore I am," or, "I am being believed in, therefore I believe." We must ask, therefore, what this self-evidencing content of revelation is and how it comes to us through the historical event. Our definitions so far have been rough circumscriptions of the context in which we look for the meaning of the word and in which the significant phrase performs its meaning-giving function. Now we must turn to the illuminating event and the intelligible word, endeavoring to point out as precisely as we can the source of the light, the meaning of the word and the self-evidencing quality of light and word.

As we make this attempt we remind ourselves of the relative standpoint we occupy in history and faith. We are not trying to describe a common human certainty gained in a common human experience; yet on the other hand we are not seeking to set forth a private and mystic assurance which is not subject to the criticism of our community, that is of all those who occupy the same standpoint and look in the same direction toward the same reality to which we look as individuals. Assurance that we are not mistaken in our ultimate convictions is not to be gained without social corroboration, but it is not to be gained either from consultation with those who, occupying a different point of view, look in a different direction and toward other realities than we do in our history and faith. Assurance grows out of immediate perception plus social corroboration and out of neither one of these alone. We also recall to mind that the definition of revelation is a social task of the historic Christian community and that we stand at a limited point in the life of that community. Our effort to define grows out of a struggle with the problem in the past; it is one effort among many others in the present and it leads into future phases of a continuing conversation. Any present definition of the central element will need to be tested by an historical theology which will examine whether it is implicit in the theology of the past, above all in the classic source, the Scriptures; it will need to be tested by systematic theology which will develop from this starting point a Christian reasoning about God, man and human destiny, and by an ethical theology which will undertake to see in how far the world's behavior can be understood and Christian response guided when this definition of revelation is made the point of departure. Above all the test of our definitions is practical—in a worship formed and reformed about this center and in a preaching informed by the conviction set forth in our definitions. No Christian can undertake at any time to define *the* meaning of revelation in any other way than this, if revelation really be the first thing in our community's life, the point from which we proceed and to which we must always go back in thought and deed.

With these limitations and relations in mind we turn to the central event with the question, "What is it that we are certain of as we regard the illuminating point in our history and how do we become certain of it?" We might state the question in terms of conceptual thought, asking, "What is the central idea in the invincible convincement that grows out of our memory of this event, or what is the unassailable proposition that is communicated and that we intuit in the presence of the historic occasion?" But idea and proposition are not the right terms to employ here. The most important fact about the whole approach to revelation to which we are committed by the acceptance of our existential situation, of the point of view of faith living in history, is that we must think and speak in terms of persons. In our history we deal with selves, not with concepts. Our universals here are not eternal objects ingredient in events but eternal persons active in particular occasions; our axioms in this participating knowledge are not self-evident convictions about the relations of such objects but certainties about fundamental, indestructible relations between persons. We need, therefore, to put our question in the following form, "What persons do we meet in the revelatory event and what convictions about personal relations become our established principles in its presence?"

When we raise the question in this way we understand why in referring to the historic event we have had to speak of revelation from the beginning rather than of discovery or vision. The only word

in our vocabulary which does justice to the knowledge of persons or selves is "revelation." Our
knowledge of other persons differs from our
knowledge of objects externally regarded not only
by being directed toward different aspects of
reality but also by being a relationship between
different terms. In objective knowledge the self is
the only active being; it does the knowing; it brings
to bear upon its object the concepts and hypotheses
in its mind. In experimentation it manipulates the
object; in evaluation it employs its own standard
of measurement. To all the intents and purposes of
the knower the object is a passive and dead thing.
This is true even when objective knowledge is directed toward human individuals or communities.
Human bodies cannot be regarded by such science
as essentially different from other animal bodies,
nor the latter as wholly distinct from inanimate
bodies. The genius of the objective approach requires that no miracle or discontinuity be posited
at the points where the inorganic merges into the
organic, the vital into the mental and the mental
into the moral. No distinction in kind is permissible
between the methods whereby uniformities of behavior are discovered in the behavior of atoms or of
thoughts. The most minute events in space and
time, though they take place in the human brain,
cannot be regarded as different in kind from the
most majestic manifestations in the cosmos. In all

such knowledge the knower is the doer; he asks the questions which are to be answered; he judges the answers; he probes into nature's secrets and discovers what was hidden. This knower, too, is essentially impersonal. He cannot really say of himself, "I think, therefore I am," but must rather say, "Thinking goes on in me but that same thinking may and must go in any other brain so related to such objects." Disinterestedness is required of such science and disinterestedness means abstraction from all personal concerns together with supreme interest in the relations of objects.

In the knowledge of other selves both the relationship and the related terms are different. This knowledge does not run from a subject to an object but from the other to the self and back again. We cannot know here save as we are known. We cannot be the *doers* but must first suffer knowledge of ourselves. To know a knower is to begin with the activity of the other who knows us or reveals himself to us by his knowing activity. No amount of initiative on our part will serve to uncover the hidden self-activity. It must make itself manifest or it cannot be known. Selves cannot be discovered as America was found by Columbus, by sailing in the direction of a secret and a guess; this new continent must come to us or remain unknown. No deductions or inductions here can lead to certainty. Knowledge of other selves must be received and responded to. Where there is no response it is evident that there is no knowledge, but our activity is the second and not the first thing. One cannot know a lover by any activity of one's own love nor a hater by any exercise of hate. Loving and hating selves must reveal themselves—penetrate through the mask of eyes and bodies; before the merely inquisitive gaze they retreat into infinite distance. Selves are known in act or not at all. Martin Buber, more than any other thinker of our object-obsessed time, has analyzed this relationship for us in his significant book, *I and Thou*. "The *Thou*," he writes, "meets me through grace—it is not found by seeking. . . . The *Thou* meets me. But I step into direct relation to it. Hence the relationship means being chosen and choosing, suffering and action in one." Meeting with such a Thou, the I is changed. The self which is known by another and so knows itself through another's eyes is not an impersonal process of thinking. It is a person with a definite character, just this particular self; it is a self which can no longer retreat infinitely behind its actions but is caught fast and held in the act of the other's knowing of it. The self which is known and so achieves self-knowledge is a committed self —an I which must acknowledge what it is and so accept itself. Such meetings with others are events in our history through which we not only know but become what we are. A meeting with an incarnate self is an event of different character from all our isolated surmises, fears, dreamings and wishes about ideal companions or enemies; after such meetings we can never again return to the self-existence which was ours before the meeting.

Because the knowledge which we gain in our history from the critical event is of this order, a knowledge for men of flesh and blood as Unamuno has it, or, in more idealistic language, a knowledge of spiritual selves, therefore we must speak of revelation. But what person is it who reveals himself in our history in such fashion that we gain a certainty which forces us to seek an intelligible unity in all our life as selves?

In popular theology in which we do not ask difficult questions or face ultimate problems the answer is usually given in terms of the person of Jesus Christ or of human personality. The central certainty we derive from our view of the historic scene, it is said, is that persons are infinitely valuable or that Jesus is the worthy person to follow. In connection with the latter answer we remind ourselves of all the emphasis on the historic person and all the appeal for personal following of Jesus which has characterized modern faith. So too for many early Christians it may be that Jesus was god and that their certainty was simply this—that they had met a person to whom they could be wholly devoted and who made persons of them.

Such thinking and preaching emphasizes that the effect of Jesus on men is greater than that of his teaching. He is, it is said, a life and not a purveyor of more or less original ideas about life; Christian life consists in becoming a person through association with him rather in the acceptance of creeds and laws. The evident truth in this conception lies in its retention of the fundamental personal note in faith. It manages, moreover, to keep in view the historical character of the church and the Christian. But despite its pragmatic values a definition of revelation in terms of the person of Jesus is manifestly inadequate. The problems which it raises are insuperable. How can we have personal communion with one who exists only in our memory and in the monuments, the books and sentences, which are the body of our memory? How can the letter and the document become a carrier of personal life unless they are part of the expressive body of a now living spirit? When we pursue this inquiry we are inclined to say that the living being with which we can have fellowship is really the church of Jesus or the spirit of the church. The latter becomes the real incarnation of the person of Jesus and faith is directed toward the community itself. What is revealed in our history, at the decisive point, is not the person of Jesus but the fellowship of the church. By a further development of this way of thought the Jesus of our history becomes the symbolic representative and product of the church; the story of his life not less than his death and resurrection, his ethical teachings as well as his eschatology, are regarded as expressions of the early church's mind. But this way lies disaster. The self-worship of non-Christian communities is enough to warn us that communal self-exaltation is an evil imagination of the heart leading to destruction of others and the self. Moreover, it is evident that if this interpretation of the central meaning of the critical historic event be true then there has been no revelation at all in our history, but only a self-knowledge on the part of the community; and such knowledge remains a very dubious thing, since it always magnifies the love and goodness of a society which to every other view is as untrustworthy as are all other human groups.

The tendency to convert concentration on the historic Jesus into concentration on the church is an indication of the fact that the definition of revelation as the self-disclosure of Jesus is rationally and morally inadequate. Unless we have another certainty prior to the certainty about Jesus' personal value the latter is very tenuous and uncertain. The fate of Jesus was like that of all persons we know. He died; and his death, being that of one we value highly, is even more disillusioning than the death of other persons. If the last certainty we have is that Jesus was the greatest of persons, then we may have a certainty beyond this one, that persons do not belong to the real structure of things in this world, that self-consciousness is illusory, that all this internal life of ours, this sense of other selves, of personal values and of our duration, are not indications of anything abiding. We must conclude that the external view affords us the only knowledge possible of dependable things and we must make our reckoning with a great impersonal cosmos which does not know that we exist and does not care for us, as it did not care for Jesus. We must conclude that we are not only mistaken in seeking the explanation of our personal existence in this or that egoistic or communal imagination but also in believing that there is any meaning at all in the existence of selves. Whatever route we follow from an original definition of our certainty in terms of Jesus' worth or person ends in uncertainty about him and about ourselves.

We must come to a similar conclusion if we say that the central certainty of Christianity is the conviction that human selves have infinite or sacred value. In a limited sense the statement is doubtless correct though when it is converted into the proposition that individuals have intrinsic worth it is either a thoroughly idolatrous, self-deifying confession of faith, a wild imagination of the heart, or

wholly loose and ambiguous. It cannot be true that
the proposition about the infinite worth of persons
is self-evident unless there be some infinite being
to whom they are valuable. It is evidently not true
if value means valency, for nothing is more evident than the weakness of selves in the immense
world of impersonal facts; and if it be maintained
that this infinite worth is a demand of the valuing
mind then the weakness of the valuing mind and
its demands in our world obtrudes itself into view.
In the reasoning of the head, dealing with things,
the demand for rationality in the world of facts
would be a quickly defeated, ever uncertain demand, if objective reality did not reveal a reason
in itself corresponding to the reason in the mind
and able to instruct it. We could not maintain the
worth of the pure reason if we knew it only in ourselves nor could it be called back from all its errant
ways if there were no objective reason. So all the
sense of personal worth which men may conceive
would remain a vain thing, and in the particular
forms in which they conceive it, an errant thing,
if it were not duplicated in and corrected by something beyond themselves. It is very true that recognition of the infinite value of souls is a concomitant
of revelation, but it could not be given were not
something else given in that event—the infinite self
for whom all souls are valuable.

When we say revelation we point to something

in the historical event more fundamental and more certain than Jesus or than self. Revelation means God, God who discloses himself to us through our history as our knower, our author, our judge and our only savior. "All revelation," Professor Herrman writes, "is the self-revelation of God. We can call any sort of communication revelation only then if we have found God in it. But we find and have God only when he so incontestably touches and seizes us that we wholly yield ourselves to him. . . . God reveals himself in that he forces us to trust him wholly." (*Der Begriff der Offenbarung*, 1887, p. 11.) One of our historical scholars sums up his inquiry into the meaning of revelation in the Scriptures in similar fashion: "Revelation is *not* the communication of supernatural knowledge and *not* the stimulation of numinous feelings. To be sure revelation can become the occasion for the growth of knowledge, and the revelation of God is necessarily accompanied by religious feelings. But revelation does not consist of these; it is the peculiar activity of God, the unveiling of his hiddenness, his giving of himself in communion." (*Theologisches Woerterbuch zum Neuen Testament*, Vol. III, p. 575.)

Revelation means the moment in our history through which we know ourselves to be known from beginning to end, in which we are apprehended by the knower; it means the self-disclosing of that eternal knower. Revelation means the moment in which we are surprised by the knowledge of someone there in the darkness and the void of human life; it means the self-disclosure of light in our darkness. Revelation is the moment in which we find our judging selves to be judged not by ourselves or our neighbors but by one who knows the final secrets of the heart; revelation means the self-disclosure of the judge. Revelation means that we find ourselves to be valued rather than valuing and that all our values are transvaluated by the activity of a universal valuer. When a price is put upon our heads, which is not our price, when the unfairness of all the fair prices we have placed on things is shown up; when the great riches of God reduce our wealth to poverty, that is revelation. When we find out that we are no longer thinking him, but that he first thought us, that is revelation. Revelation is the emergence of the person on whose external garments and body we had looked as objects of our masterful and curious understanding. Revelation means that in our common history the fate which lowers over us as persons in our communities reveals itself to be a person in community with us. What this means for us cannot be expressed in the impersonal ways of creeds or other propositions but only in responsive acts of a personal character. We acknowledge revelation by no third person proposition, such as that there is a God, but only in the direct confession of the heart, "Thou art my God." We can state the convincement given in the revelatory moment only in a prayer saying, "Our Father." Revelation as the self-disclosure of the infinite person is realized in us only through the faith which is a personal act of commitment, of confidence and trust, not a belief about the nature of things. When we speak of revelation we mean that moment when we are given a new faith, to cleave to and to betray, and a new standard, to follow and deny. Now when we fail in faith, we fail in this faith; and when we transgress, it is this person we transgress against; when we reason falsely it is in violation of the first principle given in this event. All this, since it is in our history, is part of what we are and does not belong to a serial past. It is our past in our present. From this point forward we must listen for the remembered voice in all the sounds that assail our ears, and look for the remembered activity in all the actions of the world upon us. The God who reveals himself in Jesus Christ is now trusted and known as the contemporary God, revealing himself in every event; but we do not understand how we could trace his working in these happenings if he did not make himself known to us through the memory of Jesus Christ; nor do we know how we should be able to interpret all the words we read as words of God save by the aid of this Rosetta stone.

The definition of revelation as divine self-disclosure must call forth many questions in our mind. Among these two seem to be of especial importance. We ask ourselves whether this is really what we mean in view of the fact that we have used and do use the word as designating certain truths and moral standards which are connected with the historic event. In Protestantism revelation has been commonly set forth as meaning Scriptures or its doctrinal content, such as that Jesus Christ was the Son of God, or that God forgives sin, while in Roman Catholicism revelation is always discussed as though it meant a supernatural knowledge about man's supernatural end. Moreover, we must ask ourselves whether the revelation of God as person is not so mystic an event that it becomes wholly separate from and irrelevant to our discursive knowledge and to our moral standards. A second question arises in many forms, but perhaps most frequently as the question about the meaning of the word God in this connection. If we say that revelation means divine self-disclosure we seem to infer that we can recognize God in revelation, which implies a previous knowledge of him. Is it really possible then to begin with revelation? Must we not go back of this self-disclosure to some previous knowledge of God, to an original or a general revelation, or to some ideal of God, some value-concept or other demand of reason through which we are enabled to recognize the historical event as a realization of the ideal? These are serious questions which we cannot dismiss, and it may be that in trying to answer them we shall be able to reach greater clarity about the meaning of revelation for us.

II. *Revelation and the Moral Law*

We can approach our first problem by way of some standard definitions of revelation. The Council of Trent defined the content of the Gospel as the "saving truth and moral discipline" which Jesus promulgated and which is contained in the Holy Scriptures. The Vatican Council declared that God may be known "by the natural light of human reason, by means of created things" but that it pleased God in his wisdom and bounty to reveal *"himself and the eternal decrees of his will"* by another and supernatural way. It proceeded then to speak of truths which, though not beyond reason, are nevertheless made available to faith through revelation as well as to refer also to the knowledge of man's supernatural end which is given through revelation alone. Protestant confessions of faith refer in similar manner to truths and moral laws which, along with God himself, are the content of revelation. The Westminster Confession states that, "Although the light of nature and the works of creation and providence, do so far manifest the goodness, wisdom and power of God, as to leave men inexcusable; yet are they not sufficient to give that knowledge of God, and of His will, which is necessary unto salvation; therefore it pleased the Lord, at sundry times, and in diverse manners, *to reveal himself and to declare his will* unto the church; and afterwards for the better preserving and propagating of the truth, and for the more sure establishment and comfort of the church against the corruption of the flesh, and the malice of Satan and of the world, to commit the same wholly unto writing which maketh the Holy Scripture to be most necessary; these former ways of God revealing his will unto his people being now ceased." Lutheran creeds are less insistent on the revelation of divine will than of divine favor, yet they speak of the grace of God also in terms of a revealed truth, for the content of the 'Gospel, the Augsburg Confession states, is "that God, not for our merit's sake, but for Christ's sake, doth justify those who believe that they, for Christ's sake, are received into favor." The Formula of Concord, seeking to do justice to the law, states, "We believe, teach, and confess that the Law is properly a doctrine divinely revealed, which teaches what is just and acceptable to God, and which also denounces whatever is sinful and opposite to the divine will."

In other confessions and creeds, in the writings of

the theologians and in the Scriptures also, the same duality in the concept of revelation is manifest. Upon the one hand, God reveals himself in Christ; on the other hand, Moses, the prophets and Jesus reveal the will of God and truths about his nature. Perhaps the double meaning of revelation is most evident in the Fourth Gospel in which Jesus is now presented as the Logos who teaches the truth about a God, unknowable in himself and now as the one through whom God revealed himself. "No man hath seen God at any time," writes John, "the only begotten Son, which is in the bosom of the Father, he hath declared him." But in another connection he lets Jesus assert that whoever has seen him has seen the Father. This dualism is sometimes explained as the result of the double Hellenistic and Jewish background of Christianity. As an early Christian, John speaks of the immediate knowledge of God which comes to the Christian through his self-revelation in Jesus Christ; as a Hellenistic thinker he speaks of the inferential knowledge about ultimate being which can be gained through knowledge of the Logos. But it is significant that while the Greek Christian may need to speak of both God and truth, the Jewish Christian must also speak of two things—of the person and of the knowledge of his will which revelation makes available. Whether we approach our history as Jews who seek to know the content of the divine will or as Greeks who inquire into the nature of God, in either case the question, concerning the relation of our knowledge about God to our knowledge of God himself, is a real one. On the one hand, a revelation which discloses God's self appears to be empty and incommunicable, on the other hand, knowledge of the nature and the will of God separate from the knowledge of God himself may be only a knowledge of traditional concepts and customs which are dignified with the name of revelation. The two things belong together as the confessions seem to insist, but how they belong together is not indicated in them.

Perhaps we may be assisted to a solution of the difficulty and to an answer to the various questions which arise in this connection if we approach the subject again through an analysis of our memory. We carry in our personal memory the impress of moral laws; in our social memory no less there are the long traditions of what ought and ought not to be done. As the latter tradition is embodied in laws, constitutions and institutions available to the external view, so the former doubtless has its physical counterpart in the structure, the neural pattern of our organism. In both cases the external view does not understand these laws as we do from within. When we are personally and communally identified with them, when they are our principles, when they are in our memory, then they are not simply prescriptions of behavior given by an external law-giver but our own imperatives which we can disobey only at the cost of inner conflict and suffering, which we can deny only by giving up ourselves. They are for us illuminators of our way, guardians of the path of life. They admonish us and keep us or by them we admonish and guard ourselves. But when we ask ourselves about the true source of these "Thou shalt" and "Thou shalt nots," or of these scales of values we are baffled. They seem so august and majestic that sometimes we refer them to a heavenly pronouncement, to revelation as the great miracle which accounts for all otherwise unaccountable convictions in our lives.

But such a view is challenged. Many philosophers tell us that the laws in our memory which we must bring to bear on ever new experiences are intuitions or reminiscences derived from a sphere of existence non-temporal and non-spatial in character. They ask us to dig deeply down into our inner life where we will find them recorded as the great intuitions of a transcendent reason. The ultimate laws which we remember as citizens of another, intelligible world are not the detailed statutes we have devised for our lower stages of existence in space and time; but in a loftier region the soul has heard one or two or more great commandments; there it has seen the last and highest good or the whole host of glorious values; this vision it can never forget without forgetting itself. By means of Socratic reminiscence, or through Kantian analysis, or by recollecting with Hartmann the direct vision of insubstantial yet subsistent values we are enabled to make explicit the transcendent moral laws; with these we then proceed into the daily world of work and strife, making our lesser statutes.

Historians of culture, sociologists and genetic psychologists, on the other hand, look on the behavior guided or judged by such laws, and regard them in their literal, habitual and institutional embodiments as things existing in space and time. They search for origins not in the depths of personal memory but rather in the retreating sequence of events in external history. They note how these commandments are inscribed into the habits of children by the approvals and disapprovals of their elders and companions. They trace back to the history of nomadic tribes and to their conditions of life the moral laws of the Hebrews, to the urban, aesthetic, technical, aristocratic civilization of the Greeks the spiritual scale of values and knowledge of the good. Historians follow the genealogy of the noble utterances of the Sermon on the Mount to a Rabbinic, prophetic, and pre-prophetic ancestry and find their individual differences due to life in the environment of an apocalyptic hope. There is no need to account for these moral laws by reference to any miracle of revelation. So also the kingdom-of-God ideals of modern Protestants may be traced to the social conditions of a late capitalistic time and of an early democratic enthusiasm, as original Protestantism's insistence on liberty and responsibility can be accounted for by its connections with early capitalism and a late feudalism. It may be possible indeed to indulge the over-belief that behind the long and painful history of human moral laws there is some inclusive purpose; but we cannot know, since no first purpose comes into appearance but only the interminable and knotted chain of human purposings.

It is not the task of a confessional theology to try to reconcile the differences of philosophers and sociologists, save as they are confessors, though one may venture to hazard the opinion that they are looking on the same process from divergent points of view and that strife is due to the confusion of views of the universal with universal views and to the totalitarian tendency which inclines us to believe that our outlook yields not only truth but all the truth there is. As for ourselves we cannot but accept the criticisms made of us by both groups when we refer our laws to special revelation. We recognize that they were written on our hearts apart from revelation and on our statute books without the aid of Scriptures. With Socrates we must do homage to them as laws of our society which nurtures us and which is to be obeyed more

reverently than parents are. We must agree with
the prophets who always presupposed that Israel
knew what was good, and with St. Paul who believed that the Gentiles who knew not God had
knowledge of his law in their conscience. Expressing the idea in temporal terms we can say that our
moral ideas and ideals in Western society had their
origin in events and experiences which antedate the
appearance and teaching of Jesus as well as of Moses
and the prophets. Speaking more mystically or
idealistically we confess that a knowledge of values
and intuitions of duty come to us in visions which
are not mediated by Jesus Christ in our history. If
we make our self-analysis in social terms we must
say that we achieve understanding of the requirements of life through membership in other communities than the Christian church. In general,
then, Kant seems to be right; we know an act to
be our duty before we know it to be the will of
God. Our standard creeds seem to be mistaken
when they define knowledge of the moral law as
part of revelation's content.

Yet this result leaves us unsatisfied. It is compatible with the idea of revelation as divine self-
disclosure, but also with the idea of revelation as
an unrelated and illusory element in life and with
the substitution of a postulated for a revealed God.
And neither of these alternatives represents what
we mean in our confession. Kant's analysis of his

moral consciousness does not represent the self-analysis of the Christian confessor. In the first place there is no way we know of deducing the certainty of deity's existence from the presence of the moral law in us. On this point Sidgwick seems more honest than the honest Kant. How can we reach the conclusion that there is a universal deity from the imperative of a moral law which we know—however absolute it be for us—is afflicted with the relativity of our historical reason, of our interest in the maintenance of selves and of our wishfulness for the preservation and victory of this particular individual or social self? Uncertainty about deity remains our lot when this approach is made. The deity we can deduce from moral law is no more absolute than that moral law and no more unified than we know it to be. Intimations of an existence beyond moral law we may have, but they are intimations and a great yearning only.

In the second place Kant's analysis is not an accurate description of Christian experience in its suggestion that the recognition of the moral law as the will of God, or that revelation of the person behind the moral law, leaves the latter unchanged. It is in the change which comes upon moral law with revelation of the person of God in Jesus Christ that an indication is given of the way in which the definition of revelation in the creeds must be maintained, yet the dualism between revelations of a person and of his will overcome. In so far as our analysis of this change is accurate a test of the definition of revelation as the disclosure of God's self will have been successfully met.

The first change which the moral law undergoes with the revelation of God's person is in its imperativeness. When God reveals himself the moral law no longer states what we demand of ourselves in order that we may become what we ought to be; from this demand we can escape by asking why we ought to be anything else than we are. It no longer states what the best reason of the best men demands, a requirement which may also be evaded through our doubt of reason's power and of the goodness of our best reasoners. Nor does it continue to convey the demand of our society, which we can avoid by getting out of our society; now it is not just the decree of life from which we may take refuge in voluntary or involuntary death. Through the revelation of God the moral law is known as the demand of one from whom there is no flight, who respects no persons, and makes no exceptions, whose seriousness of purpose will not suffer that his work be destroyed by the evasions and transgressions of this pitiful, anarchic creature who sets up his little kingdoms in rebellion against God's sovereignty, and proclaims ever new Messiahs to lead him to new disasters in the name of his own righteousness. Transgressions of our law no longer appear as acts which go against the grain of our nature, or of our social, or biological life; to be sure they do all these things, but primarily they go against the grain of the universe. Transgressions do not merely break the law of conscience or of our society or even of life, but the law of the beginner and perfecter of all that is. They do not merely violate the soul and body of the self or its community; they do violence to the body of God; it is his son who is slain by our iniquity. There is no escape from the judgment of that transgression or from the necessity of making good that violation through any hope of forgetfulness on his part or through a death which would remove us from his sphere. The imperative behind the law is the imperative of the faithful, earnest, never-resting, eternal self. As the prophets did not declare to Israel a new morality but directed attention to the eternal imperative behind a nomadic morality, so Jesus Christ gives us, first of all, no new ethics but reveals the lawgiver whose implacable will for the completion and redemption of his creation does not allow even his most well beloved son to exempt himself from the suffering necessary to that end. The righteousness of God which is revealed in Jesus Christ is the eternal earnestness of a personal God.

The moral law is changed, furthermore, by the revelation of God's self in that its evermore extensive and intensive application becomes necessary. There is no possibility now of so confining the law to a people that duty to the neighbor is duty to a blood-brother only, or that an explicit act is more subject to ethical judgment than the implicit movements which occur within the privacy of the individual organism, in the brain, in the body. Nor can the will of God be interpreted so that it applies within a world of rational beings and not in the world of the unrational, so that men must be treated as ends because they are reasonable but non-human life may be violated in the service of human ends. Sparrows and sheep and lilies belong within the network of moral relations when God reveals himself; now every killing is a sacrifice. The line cannot even be drawn at the boundaries of life; the culture of the earth as a garden of the Lord and reverence for the stars as creatures of his intelligence belong to the demands of the universal will. There is no possibility now of restricting moral obedience to the circle of the good, so that we love those who love us or who share our principles and do no harm to our values. Loyalty to the soul of the enemy, not only of our life but of our higher goods, becomes imperative when God, not life or reason or moral value, issues the commandment. In time as in space and social relations the moral law that is a law of God is extended and intensified. It is the law of a living contemporary being, new in every new moment and therefore forever changing in its specific form. No merely traditional way of doing things is right in the presence of the living authority. What is commanded by God is commanded anew in every new moment for that moment, though the faithfulness of the will binds all the moments together and gives abiding direction amid the novelties of changing days.

When our moral law is universalized and intensified in this fashion it is reborn. The limitations which circumscribed our law as Hebrews are overcome, and the barriers are shattered which confined our ethical requirements and possibilities as Greeks to men of intellectual reason and gave it an academically aristocratic character. So also this revelation must erase the boundaries of all the successive moralities, of Christendom as of Jewry and paganism. When God becomes the will behind the moral law a great process of levelling takes place; all the mountains are brought low and the valleys are all exalted. A revolutionary transvaluation occurs not in addition to the personal revelation but because of it. It may be better to say that a restoration is begun, for in the presence of the person we recognize that the moral law, as we had entertained it, was always a corrupted thing, that there never was in our conscience, in our philosophies, or on our statute books a law which was not in the service of some deity. No matter what standard of measurement we employed—whether that of perfection, or that of pleasure—or what intuition of benevolence or prudence we used, we used these laws and measures as interested men, who served a creature rather than the creator. If we used pleasure as our standard for measuring the good, it was *our* pleasure or *my* pleasure which was preferred. If it was perfection, then it was *our* perfection; if prudence was our law it was a prudence in the service of a larger or a smaller self, and if benevolence was our intuition, it was a benevolence for those of our own kind, from whom we might expect some return of our kindness. We were and are unable to achieve the single-mindedness of impersonal science in our moral thinking and acting not because we could and can not be impersonal here but because we would and will not look at things from the viewpoint of a universal person. It is always an interested morality, a wishful and idolatrous and corrupted one which we employ apart from God.

This great corruption of our values, standards and our moral laws is made most evident by a revelation in which we know ourselves as we are known. Revelation points the moral law at us, saying, "Thou art the man." In this light we know that we have used the law in service of self and in this use always corrupted it. We pride ourselves, as Jews, Greeks, Christians, democrats, socialists or nationalists upon our moral law, as though it were a thing that could be possessed otherwise than in act. We justify ourselves before men as churches and as other groups because of the nobility of our ideals. We disguise our transgressions by a vast self-deceit, and when the law too obviously disagrees with our wishes and vices we correct it, inventing new moralities, designed not to make possible the performance of our duty but its evasion. Then we call our greed the sacred right of liberty, our covetousness liberation from slavery, our economic warfare peace, our sentimentalities love, our callousness scientific attitude, our isolation love of peace, our wars crusades, our unwillingness to accept responsibility monasticism, our compromises churchmanship. And our workaday self-justification and self-deception is given academic rationalization in theological and philosophical treatises bearing the titles of "Christian Ethics" and "Moral Philosophy." In the light of revelation we discern the elevation and the degradation of our moral laws. Revelation of the person, then, is not revelation of the law but of the law's sin and so a criticism of the law as well as its validation.

Of the greatest change which comes upon the law through God's revelation in Jesus Christ we must say very little though it is the greatest change. The conversion of the imperative into an indicative and of the law whose content is love into a free love of God and man is the possibility which we see through revelation. Even more than in the case of the other aspects of the reborn law we discern this feature as a potentiality rather than as actuality, as a promise of what the law shall be for us when the great travail of historic life is past. Yet the discernment of the promise is the beginning of a new understanding of the law and the beginning of a new life.

So the revelation of the person may be said to involve the republication of the moral law. But what is republished is an original edition that had been hopelessly corrupted by a multitude of wretched translators and conceited scholars of whom we Christians doubtless are the worst. It is better, however, to dismiss the old parable of republication which the Deists and Supernaturalists of static societies have used and abused so long. The original edition of the moral law is not handed to us in definitive form through any act of revelation. Let us rather say that when the lawgiver is revealed with his intentions the reasoning heart is granted the rudiments of a scholarly equipment by means of which, with much pain and labor, it may through all its history work at the restoration of the fundamental text. That this reason will often be led astray by evil imaginations and that it will introduce new corruptions is also certain in the light of a revelation which shows up man's sinful self even as it discloses the personal goodness of God.

In this sense a revelation which is primarily self-disclosure includes knowledge of "divine decrees" or of the will of God. The latter is not an immediate content of revelation as though God imparted to men, apart from their reasoning, new imperatives or moral truths otherwise unknown. In loose usage we may extend the term revelation to cover the reconstruction of the moral law but if we would speak accurately we must say that revelation is the beginning of a revolutionary understanding and application of the moral law rather than the giving of a new law.

What is true of ethics is true also of the opinions men hold about the world of nature and about history. Revelation imparts no new beliefs about natural or historical facts; it does involve the radical reconstruction of all our beliefs, since these always reflect both human provincialism and concern for self with its idols as well as objective knowledge. The story of the creation in six days is not a part of revelation; yet the account in Genesis, with its dominant interest in God and its partial displacement of man from the central place in the drama of becoming, represents at least the partial reconstruction of ancient beliefs in consequence of revelation. The reconstruction was not complete, for the revolution faith brings to belief is also permanent. It proceeds in many ways, on many different levels.

Faith in the person who creates the self, with all its world, relieves the mind of the pagan necessity of maintaining human worth by means of imaginations which magnify the glory of man. When the creator is revealed it is no longer necessary to defend man's place by a reading of history which establishes his superiority to all other creatures. To be a man does not now mean to be a lord of the beasts but a child of God. To know the person is to lose all sense of shame because of kinship with the clod and the ape. The mind is freed to pursue its knowledge of the external world disinterestedly not by the conviction that nothing matters, that everything is impersonal and valueless, but by the faith that nothing God has made is mean or unclean. Hence any failure of Christians to develop a scientific knowledge of the world is not an indication of their loyalty to the revealed God but of their unbelief. A genuinely disinterested science may be one of the greatest affirmations of faith and all the greater because it is so unconscious of what it is doing in this way. Resistance to new knowledge about our earthly home and the journey of life is never an indication of faith in the revealed God but almost always an indication that our sense of life's worth rests on the uncertain foundations of confidence in our humanity, our society, or some other evanescent idol. But this is not to say that new opinions about the nature of the world can in any sense be called revelation. The idea of an emergent evolution may be developed by a mind freed from the necessities of defending the place of man in nature. But in itself it is no more compatible with the revelation of the person of God than any other idea. The only question we can raise about such opinions is whether or not they are true to the course of events as we see them without fear or passion. And deliverance from fear and passion does not come to us through the knowledge of nature without the knowledge of God.

The situation is not different when we deal with opinions about the way in which our Christian community or Jesus Christ were born after the flesh and about their histories. Revelation of the person of God through Jesus Christ does not include the communication of the propositions that Jesus was born of a Virgin, that the Scriptures are inerrant, and that history is catastrophic. It does make necessary a transformation of the opinion that Jesus was only a carpenter's son, or an illegitimate child as some Jews asserted, that the Bible is another book like all the others that men write, and that human history is just another cycle of seasons. Revelation requires us to read the story of Jesus' birth like the story of life's beginnings, with God in the center of the story. It is his action we are attending to. But when we have conceived faith in him, or rather when by his revelation of himself he brings forth faith in us, we are freed from the necessity of putting our confidence in a natural miracle of birth, or a natural miracle of authorship. We are set free to trace the external course of events without fear or passion just because we have been given confidence in the author of those events. Here we verge once more on the problem of the relations of the external to the internal view which cannot be pursued in this connection. This, however, seems to be the consequence of the revelation of the person—truth is transformed and the search for continuous relations in the world which contemplative reason views is expedited and liberated. The pure reason does not need to be limited in order that room be made for faith, but faith emancipates the pure reason from the necessity of defending and guarding the interests of selves, which are now found to be established and guarded, not by nature, but by the God of revelation whose garment nature is.

III. *Human Value and the God of Revelation*

Now the second set of difficulties which our definition of revelation must encounter rise to view. It cannot be enough to say that in revelation we meet the divine self, for if this meeting is pure immediacy which does not provide us with truths about God it would remain incommunicable and unable to provide the reasoning heart with principles of understanding. A social mysticism may be ineffable in the language of another society but wholly ineffable it cannot be if it is social. Moreover, the confession of faith in the revealed self, as our God, implies some previous knowledge of what deity is; otherwise the God of revelation could not be recognized as God. In the third place, it appears that we have religious knowledge apart from revelation in our history since we can speak about God with members of non-Christian communities, not only with Jews whose memories we largely have made our own but with Mohammedans and Hindus, using words which appear to have some common meaning. Hence we must ask ourselves whether revelation of God himself in Jesus Christ is really our first principle, the starting point of our thinking and of our worship, or whether there is not a natural knowledge of God prior, in time and in the logic of our hearts, to revelation. This is an ancient puzzle for Christians and its solution has not been aided by the use of rival theories for defense and attack in the conflict between a mundane church and the world, in the wars of religion and in the strife of parties in the Christian community.

Confessional theology must approach the problem with the resolution to restrain its desire to prove the superiority of Christianity to other religions or of a Christian theology to philosophy by pointing to the church's possession of revelation. The revelation of God is not a possession but an event, which happens over and over again when we remember the illuminating center of our history. What we can possess is the memory of Jesus Christ, but what happens to us through that memory we cannot possess. What is more important, revelation turns against the self which would defend itself; it is the happening which leaves the men to whom it happens without excuse. Hence we must approach the subject as confessors and say as honestly as we can how revelation seems to be related to our other knowledge of God.

It is true that we find religion in our whole history and life as we find moral law. We discover in ourselves many beliefs and postulates about the sources and the goals of our life. Our memory is filled with arguments for the existence of a deity which do not seem directly connected with the memory of Jesus Christ and which have their external embodiment not in Scriptures but in another literature. Plato's Form of the Good, Aristotle's unmoved mover, and the Stoic Kosmos and Logos are in our minds as ideas about the world which unite with our immediate experiences giving them form. There are older, more primitive, images in our memory. It may be that they come out of some racial unconsciousness and have their visible counterpart somewhere in the physiological structure;

or it may be that they are embodied in a never wholly suppressed primitive literature, in hidden monuments, in the veiled allusions which even the incarnations of nobler ideas—even the Scriptures—contain, or in the common language whose symbols retain, despite their frequent conversion, elements of primitive thought. Such religious words as "sacrifice," "propitiation," "regeneration," "Holy Ghost," "spiritual," "love," "fellowship," and the like symbolize still, though in suppressed form, images, ideas and experiences out of a primitive past. In our desiring nature also there are questing movements that make use of these high and low, these abstract and concrete imaginations. We yearn after a companionship in which our value as selves will be recognized, after beings which will save us from the ignominy of personal and communal defeat. In the presence of an apparently indifferent nature we seek to maintain the world of our hopes by calling to our aid forces which are able to master nature as we are not able to do. We desire that the values which we cherish in embodied form—loved companions, children, nations, and cultures—be given a guarantee of continued existence which we cannot give, and that the realization of unrealized ideals of truth, beauty and goodness be insured by a power and purpose more continuous than our own. We feel within ourselves the tremor and awe that intimate the presence of beings different in power and character from those we meet in too familiar surroundings. When nature, become too familiar, can no longer cast the spell of the numinous on us, when the pageantry and power of societies has revealed itself as hollow show or as destructive demonry, we seek emancipation from the sense of the barren waste of life in music and in color. We attend the places of official worship to let the symbols of an ancient faith work on us, we know not how. Adoration, prayer, thanksgiving, intercession—these are our daily rites. From these experiences of ours we turn back to the images of mind and heart, to the abstract ideas of our philosophies, seeking to understand our natural religion.

Philosophers of the inner life analyze for us these ideas and desires and sometimes seek to justify them to us. They show us how we cannot think at all about our world save as something with a beginning and end, a cosmos issuing from a sufficient reason and tending toward a sufficient goal. When they take seriously our sense of values and of moral law they include for us in the sufficient cause a source of value, and in the end a being who unites worthiness to exist with existence. Back of all other arguments for the existence of a deity, they indicate, there lies the importunate demand of the practical reason for a reality which will conserve selves with their values, be these other selves, or impersonal and abstract goods such as beauty, truth and goodness. If the life of selves with their devotion to ends worthy of selves is real, then there ought to be a deity, and what his nature ought to be can also be described. In order that all the other values, all the little gods for whom men live, may be insured against mortality there ought to be a *Juppitter Optimus Maximus*. In order that our lives may not be mistaken quests after phantom goods this deity ought to be one, eternal, omnipresent, omnipotent, immutable, immense, incomprehensible, without body, parts or passions.

From another point of view psychologists, historians and sociologists regard our religious behavior and undertake to show us its nature and its sources. These numinous feelings are of the same sort that men experience in all frustrations. The projections into the world of purposes and animae are characteristic of primitive metaphysics and naïve science. Propitiatory and atoning rites have their source in fear and in primitive conceptions of the nature of blood and life. Sex and hunger have left their marks on every expression of faith. By and large, religion has its source in human nature and it is necessary to study man if we would know his gods. In large part our natural religion arises out of our social effort to keep in check the anarchic, individualistic, centrifugal tendencies in society. Its archaic language indicates its conservative social function and its conceptions reflect the social interest. Heavenly kings are the imaginative counterparts of earthly rulers and divine law is the projection of social custom; the distinctions between castes and groups are referred to supernatural origins in order that they may be maintained on earth. Back of all these natural faiths lies the fear of death, of loss of goods and the desire for self-maintenance and extension. Man conceives and brings forth the gods in his own image in order that his image of himself may be protected. Religion is the great self-defense of man against natural and social change; but its defensive use sometimes calls for offensive tactics, as when it is employed to drug a man's or a group's human opponents with promises of after-life and bliss.

As in the case of ethics we need to accept both accounts of the relations of our religious beliefs to subjective and objective factors, though with the recognition that each envisions limited aspects of experience and reality and also with the elimination of all totalitarian "nothing-but" phrases. In either case our thoughts about deity's nature do not need to be referred to a source in special revelation. Though they cannot therefore be regarded as non-historical and simply rational, our ideas of the goodness, omnipotence and eternity of deity represent the demand of our Western, Hellenized, human reason and come to us in social memories which are not connected with the name of and life of Christ.

This general result is compatible with the conclusion that revelation means divine self-disclosure rather than communication of truths about God. But it would also be compatible with the conclusion that such ideas are enough, that revelation is unnecessary and illusory, and that if it does occur in Christian history it is so empty as to be meaningless for all moments of life save the one in which it occurs. And this is not what we mean. Despite all difficulties that we have in speaking of it, revelation does not mean for us something we can do without or something that is incommunicable. It is true that revelation is not the communication of new truths and the supplanting of our natural religion by a supernatural one. But it is the fulfillment and the radical reconstruction of our natural knowledge about deity through the revelation of one whom Jesus Christ called "Father." All thought about deity now undergoes a metamorphosis. Revelation is not a development of our religious ideas but their continuous conversion. God's self-disclosure is that permanent revolution in our religious life by which all religious truths are painfully transformed and all religious behavior transfigured by repentance and new faith. It is revolutionary since it makes a new beginning and puts an end to the old development; it is permanent revolution since it can never come to an end in time in such a way that an irrefrangible knowledge about God becomes the possession of an individual or a group. Life in the presence of revelation in this respect as in all others is not lived before or after but in the midst of a great revolution.

How revelation is revolution in religious knowledge may be indicated by reference to the ideas we have about divine unity, reality and especially goodness. The unity of deity which we anticipated in our hypotheses about deity is realized in the revelation of God in Christ. Beyond the many and conditioned beings for which and among which we lived, beyond eternal objects and ideas we have learned to posit one unconditioned being. We thought about a single principle which might serve as the source of the unities we find in our experience. But though the Father of our Lord Jesus Christ met that expectation he fulfilled it in another manner than we anticipated, and made necessary a change in all our thinking about the unity of the world. He met us not as the one beyond the many but as the one who acts in and through all things, not as the unconditioned but as the conditioner. The oneness of the person was the oneness of a will directed towards unity of all things in our world. He was no Jupiter beyond the lesser gods but the enemy of these, who revealed in our efforts to find him through them a worship of idols and demons. By that revelation we discern how into all our thought about his unity we imported the idea of such special unity as we had in ourselves. He was the apex of a pyramid that we built on earthly foundations according to our own design, so that the hierarchy of heaven and earth was conceived in the image of our own nature or of our society's. But the Father of Jesus Christ does not bear the image of our unity; through him we see our disorder and our lack of unity and through him find unity flowing into our world in another manner than we desired. For him our last things are first and our first things last. As the one person in our history he demands furthermore of us not the static unity of established order but the unity of life aspiring toward and impelled by an infinite purpose. This is not the one in whom we come to rest but the one through whom life comes to us. He is the one who ties all our world together by meeting us in every event and requiring us to think his thoughts after him in every moment. God who comes to man in Jesus Christ is one, as the deity of our religious imagination is one, but he demands the reformation of every particular idea of unity we have, and the making of a new beginning in our effort to understand his nature. The doctrine of the Trinity is no satisfactory or final formulation of this understanding, but it is more satisfactory than all the ancient and the modern pantheons wherein we ascend beyond the many gods or values to someone who is limited by them. The unity of the God who appears as Father, Son and Holy

Spirit is not the unity which we conceive as the common source and spirit of beauty, truth and goodness, especially not as we conceive truth, beauty and goodness in our own image. And so the oneness which the God of Jesus Christ demands in us is not the integration of our purposes and values but our integrity, singleness of mind and purity of heart.

Revelation is no less the revolution in our thought about divine power. In order that any being may qualify as a deity before the bar of religious reason it must be good, but it must also be powerful. There may be beings we can adore for their goodness which are as powerless as the self-subsistent values and the eternal objects of modern philosophy. But what is powerless cannot have the character of deity; it cannot be counted upon, trusted in; to it no prayers ascend. When goodness and power fall apart and when we have no confidence in the power of the good or in the good of power our religion turns to magic—to the exercise of our own power whose goodness we do not doubt. Our adoration then may be directed to eternal values but our petitions descend upon congressmen and senators, who both exercise power and can be moved. Deity, whatever else it must be to be deity, must be powerful in its goodness as well as good in its power. When deity is reduced to an idea in our minds or to an ideal of the future which alone is good, then

man logically turns to self-worship and to invocations addressed to his own will. When man notes
his inability to live by his own power and the power
of everything that is against him becomes manifest,
he may be led to trust in the goodness of that which
is most evidently powerful. He may come to a Stoic
resignation to the world, to the last system of forces
he can imagine, to that vast conspiracy of natural
powers which surround him and have him at their
mercy. He has his bitter moments when he is
tempted to Promethean rebellions against things as
they are. But this world, nature, fate, the historic
process—whatever it be called—is real and he who
resigns himself to it has the consolation of knowing
that he is no longer fooling himself with imaginations and fashioning deities out of his wishful thinking. In any case the thought of deity and the
thought of power are inseparable. Deity must be
strong if it is to be deity.

We meet the God of Jesus Christ with the expectations of such power. If his power be less than
that of the world and he be at the mercy of the
world, of nature, fate and death, how shall we
recognize him as God? Yet we do not meet this
God, he comes to us through and in our human
history, fulfilling and destroying our expectations
of power. His reality and power is the reality and
power of the world. He is the one to whom Jesus
prays as the Lord of Heaven and Earth; he is the

descending rain and the shining sun, careless of the distinctions which men make between the good and evil. The God to whom Jesus is obedient to death is the life-giving and death-dealing power. And yet how strangely we must revise in the light of Jesus Christ all our ideas of what is really strong in this powerful world. The power of God is made manifest in the weakness of Jesus, in the meek and dying life which through death is raised to power. We see the power of God over the strong of earth made evident not in the fact that he slays them, but in his making the spirit of the slain Jesus unconquerable. Death is not the manifestation of power; there is a power behind and in the power of death which is stronger than death. We cannot come to the end of the road of our rethinking the ideas of power and omnipotence. We thought that we knew their meaning and find we did not know and do not know now, save that the omnipotence of God is not like the power of the world which is in his power. His power is made perfect in weakness and he exercises sovereignty more through crosses than through thrones. So with revelation we must begin to rethink all ideas about deity. We cannot help ourselves. We must make a new beginning in our thought as in our action. Revelation is the beginning of a revolution in our power thinking and our power politics.

Finally we know as members of the common

human community that deity must be good. We can achieve no Stoic resignation to the world, nor stake the meaning of our life on our devotion to a national cause, unless we can persuade ourselves that the strong reality is also worthy of loyalty. Whatever else deity may be in philosophical definition or in practical worship it must be value. The word God is a value term like the word friend. Each of these symbols represents a combination of value and being. We would not use the word God at all if all we meant were designated by the word good, but neither would we use it if we meant only power. To say that God and faith belong together is to maintain that no power could be apprehended as God save as its value were made manifest. Now the goodness we expect of deity is both intrinsic and instrumental. The gods of human devotion are in part beings who are adored for their own sakes and in part those to whom appeal is made for the protection and nurture of other intrinsic goods. In general our religion, official and unofficial, indicates its tendency toward polytheism by directing its worship to one set of beings and its prayers to another. We adore and worship that for the sake of which we live; we pray to that which is able to preserve the beings we adore. If deity is one it needs to combine with power an adorable and a ministering goodness.

It is with such demands that we enter into the moment of revelation. The God who reveals himself in Jesus Christ meets no unresponsive will but the living spirit of men in search of all good. And he fulfills our need. Here is the one for whose sake all life and every life is worth living, even lives that seem bereft of beauty, of truth and of goodness. The glimpse of his great glory in the face of Jesus Christ, its reflections in the darkened mirrors of the saints' adorations intimate a God who is good beyond all that is good and fair beyond all fairness. Yet the goodness that shines upon us through the moment of revelation is not the glory or the goodness we had expected in our thought about deity. The essential goodness of the Father of our Lord Jesus Christ is the simple everyday goodness of love —the value which belongs to a person rather the value we find in an idea or a pattern; it is the goodness which exists as pure activity. He fulfills our expectation of the intrinsic good and yet this adorable goodness differs from everything we had expected, and puts our expectations to shame. We sought a good to love and were found by a good that loved us. And therewith all our religious ambitions are brought low, all our desires to be ministers of God are humbled; he is our minister. By that revelation we are convicted of having corrupted our religious life through our unquenchable desire to keep ourselves with our love of our good in the center of the picture. Here is goodness that empties itself, and makes itself of no reputation, a goodness that is all outgoing, reserving nothing for itself, yet having all things. So we must begin to rethink all our definitions of deity and convert all our worship and our prayers. Revelation is not the development and not the elimination of our natural religion; it is the revolution of the religious life.

Our thoughts also about the goods which deity sustains are caught up in the great turmoil of a transvaluation. The self we loved is not the self God loves, the neighbors we did not prize are his treasures, the truth we ignored is the truth he maintains, the justice which we sought because it was our own is not the justice that his love desires. The righteousness he demands and gives is not our righteousness but greater and different. He requires of us the sacrifice of all we would conserve and grants us gifts we had not dreamed of—the forgiveness of our sins rather than our justification, repentance and sorrow for our transgressions rather than forgetfulness, faith in him rather than confidence in ourselves, trust in his mercy rather than sight of his presence, instead of rest an ever recurrent torment that will not let us be content, instead of the peace and joy of the world, the hope of the world to come. He forces us to take our sorrows as a gift from him and to suspect our joys lest they be purchased by the anguish of his son incarnate again in every neighbor. He ministers indeed to all our good but all our good is other than we thought.

This conversion and permanent revolution of our human religion through Jesus Christ is what we mean by revelation. Whatever other men may say we can only confess, as men who live in history, that through our history a compulsion has been placed upon us and a new beginning offered us which we cannot evade. We must say with St. Augustine: "Walk by him the man and thou comest to God. By him thou goest, to him thou goest. Look not for any way except himself by which to come to him. For if he had not vouchsafed to be the way we should all have gone astray. Therefore he became the way by which thou shouldest come. *I do not say to thee, seek the way. The way itself is come to thee: arise and walk.*"

INDEX